TREASURES

OF

TIME

**A Fully Illustrated Guide to
Prehistoric Ceramics
of the
Southwest**

A treasure trove of prehistoric ceramics
emerging sherd by sherd from Raven Site
Ruins in the White Mountains of Arizona.

by

James R. Cunkle

**GOLDEN
WEST ☼
PUBLISHERS**

Cover photos by Norman W. Mead

Text and color plate photos by author

Also by James R. Cunkle

Talking Pots — *Deciphering the Symbols of a Prehistoric People*

```
┌─────────────────────────────────────────────────────────────┐
│       Library of Congress Cataloging-in-Publication Data     │
│ Cunkle, James R.,                                            │
│     Treasures of Time: A fully illustrated guide to prehistoric ceramics of the │
│     Southwest / James R. Cunkle                              │
│         p.    cm.                                            │
│     Includes index, bibliography, glossary, 16 pages full-color plates │
│     1. Raven Site (Arizona)    2. Pueblo Pottery  3. Pottery │
│     Prehistoric — Arizona — Raven Site — Classification. 4. Pottery. │
│     Prehistoric — Arizona — Raven Site — Themes, motives. 5. Pueblo │
│     Indians — Antiquities.   I. Title.                      │
│     E99.P9C848   1994                      94-16275         │
│     738.3'09791'37—dc20                    CIP             │
└─────────────────────────────────────────────────────────────┘
```

Printed in the United States of America

ISBN #0-914846-92-2

First Printing

Golden West Publishers, Inc.
4113 N. Longview Ave.
Phoenix, AZ 85014, USA
(602) 265-4392

Dedication

To Carol,
My wife,
My friend,
and loose cannon rider.

Acknowledgments

Space restraints do not permit the acknowledgment of the army of people who have and are still devoting their time, patience and pride to the Raven Site Project. Their energy, enthusiasm and belief in the project, without a doubt, made the compilation of this ceramic guide possible.

To Markus Jacquemain and Jeff Brown: *"Wise men know we are wise."* Thank you, gentlemen.

Table of Contents

Full Color Insert is located between pages 82 and 83

Preface

This volume will present the ceramic assemblages from Raven Site Ruins, located near the city of Springerville in the White Mountains of Arizona. This material has never before been published, with the exception of the pottery vessels that exhibit meaningful iconography (Cunkle 1993). Here we will illustrate and analyze the cultural material from the site that was created from clay or used in the process of forming or finishing the clay.

We will begin with the earliest types found to date, and continue through the later ceramic types, up until the abandonment of the site around A.D. 1550. The earliest ceramic assemblages are found in the north pueblo area of Raven Site Ruins. These begin around the year A.D. 900. Even earlier assemblages may yet be discovered. The north pueblo has several occupations built on top of previous occupations, and excavators have not yet reached the lowest levels of this area of the site. These yet undiscovered lower levels will undoubtedly reveal even earlier ceramic assemblages.

The area of the south pueblo of Raven Site Ruins provides us with the later ceramics from the site as a whole. Many of these have not been thoroughly researched. They are poorly described if they have been described at all in the literature.

There does seem to be a continuation from the earlier north pueblo ceramics to the later south pueblo ceramic assemblages. These connections will be discussed type by type as we proceed through time and look at these beautiful vessels.

One of the primary purposes of this volume is to provide the reader with ceramic type descriptions, dates, the general geographical area where each type is found, the form that the vessels take on during the time of their production, and basically how to recognize one type from another. This is an important ability in archaeology of the Southwest, because each ceramic type is associated with a date when that type was produced. Simply by recognizing the ceramic type when you excavate a sherd or pick one up from an eroded surface, allows the researcher to accurately and instantly provide a date for that level, feature or area of occupation. This is certainly the quickest and least expensive dating technique in Southwestern archaeology. The accuracy of pottery typing as a dating method is surpassed by other dating techniques such as dendrochronology (tree-ring dating), obsidian hydration, etc., but it still remains as a valuable archaeological tool when combined with other relative and absolute dating methods.

You will notice that after naming each ceramic type in the sequence, the first information included is the estimated dates for that ceramic type. I have discovered that even after I have achieved proficiency in recognizing each type in the field, I still often need to refer to the record for the date.

The ceramics of the Southwest changed over time. New colors were introduced, new forms were tried and abandoned, and with each change, slowly, new ceramic types evolved. Recognizing different ceramic types and knowing when they were made is a lot like recognizing different styles of cars and knowing when they left the factory. When you see a Model A, those who know their automobiles also know that this particular style of car was produced late in the 1920s and into the early 1930s. Accurate dates can be assigned to most autos from the beginning of the century to the present, simply by recognizing if the headlights are outside the fenders or enclosed into the body, or if gaudy tail fins are present. Knowing your prehistoric ceramics is a very similar skill.

One of the most frequently asked questions that I have received from my staff here at Raven Site Ruins over our years of research and excavation is "how can I learn the different pottery types?". This is not an easy question to answer. There is no single volume, or collection of volumes that I can recommend that will clearly demonstrate the various pottery types of the Southwest in any way that would enable the reader to learn to distinguish one from the other. Most of the academic write-ups focus on a single excavation or excavation area. They usually include a black-and-white photo or two of the more abundant types found during their excavations. Most excavations in any single area reveal only a few different ceramic types. Most pueblo sites in the Southwest have brief occupational periods, that is, a short temporal depth. Consequently the ceramic assemblages are seldom complex. Most sites will exhibit only a dozen or so different ceramic types.

Even the research that has been done to classify the different ceramics into types does little to help teach this skill to others. The literature often only includes written descriptions of the types and perhaps a few sketches of sherds in black and white. It is next to impossible to learn to recognize a pottery type by reading a description of the type, and the sherd sketches are virtually useless for this purpose. Good photos are absolutely essential in order to begin to differentiate one ceramic type from another.

As we examine the pottery from Raven Site Ruins, photos will accompany the type descriptions. Some of the types that will be presented will be accompanied by only one photo showing a very small assemblage of that type. This is because some of the types that will be discussed that are critical in the sequence, have only rarely been found at Raven Site Ruins. Other ceramic types presented will be accompanied by several photos of pottery, indicating that large assemblages of this particular ceramic type have been found at Raven Site Ruins. It could be concluded that large assemblages of a particular ceramic style from Raven Site Ruins would indicate that there was greater ceramic production during the time that those types were produced, or possibly that there was a larger population at the site during that temporal period. Caution should be exercised when attempting these conclusions. Raven Site Ruins is estimated to have over 800 rooms and two distinct occupational periods. Excavators to date have un-earthed only twenty-two rooms. The assemblages that are presented may not truly represent the total ceramic assemblages yet to be discovered.

The best way to learn the various ceramic types and distinguish them from one another is to actually go to the collections held by the various institutions around the country, and physically examine the vessels. This could take you several years, because there are over 800 different ceramic types that have been classified in the Southwest. Even the best collections held by museums usually only contain a fraction of these types, and gaining access to examine and photograph the collections is often next to impossible.

Raven Site Ruins have so far revealed over 70 ceramic types. This is certainly also just a fraction of the whole known ceramic taxonomy of the Southwest, but the Raven Site Ruins ceramic collections have several teaching advantages. One of the most important teaching advantages is that these collections are open and available to anyone with a legitimate research project. They can be examined simply by calling the White Mountain Archaeological Center and requesting a time slot, with a curator, who will assist in handling and locating vessels within the collections.

The ceramics at Raven Site Ruins were produced on the site for over 800 years. This wonderful temporal depth allows us to see firsthand the small changes over time that eventually produced new ceramic types. Also, Raven Site Ruins was a major trade center along the Little Colorado River. This means that many of the ceramic types that we will examine have been traded in from hundreds of miles away. Raven Site Ruins potters were also producing ceramics to trade out. Because of this focus on exporting ceramics from the site, new ceramic methods were continually attempted, new designs and colors were tried. The differences between the ceramics produced at Raven Site Ruins and those that were produced elsewhere will be discussed. These differences are often the key to typing a ceramic vessel. Also found at Raven Site Ruins are prehistoric copies of different ceramics that were not normally produced at the site, but the Raven Site potters admired their beauty and form enough to attempt to produce something similar. Often the Raven Site Ruins copies are better that the originals, in form, firing and color.

The Raven Site Ruins ceramics fall into five primary groups: White Mountain Red Wares, Zuni Glaze Wares, Cibola White Wares, trade wares, and corrugated or cooking vessels.

It is very unusual for any ruin in the Southwest to contain the diversity of ceramic material that has been discovered at Raven Site Ruins. There are several reasons that may account for this large assemblage of different ceramics. First of all, Raven Site Ruins were occupied from as early as A.D. 800 to possibly as late as A.D. 1550. There are several different occupational periods at the site, but the site was never totally abandoned. There are populational peaks and declines. As many as two or three hundred people would occupy the site for between sixty or eighty years, diminish the surrounding resources, specifically firewood and game, and then move on to greener pastures. But not everyone moved. Several families would remain on the site. These occupational peaks and dips are evident on the site by the way different areas of the pueblo were used and re-used, over and over again. As generation after generation of peoples occupied Raven Site Ruins, the ceramics that they created evolved. New pigments were discovered, new firing techniques were tried, new slips were applied. With each new advancement (and sometimes decline) in ceramic design and technology, new ceramic types were invented. Over a span of nearly 800 years, there were dozens and dozens of changes in these ceramic assemblages.

Because these ceramic changes can be correlated with other archaeological dating techniques it is possible to assign a date to each of the ceramic types. This gives the archaeologists working at Raven Site Ruins a great advantage during their excavations. As each level of cultural material is excavated, it is possible in most cases to date these levels by using ceramic typology, often with an accuracy within fifty years or less.

Another reason why so many ceramic types are found at the site is because of the extensive trade networks that existed. Raven Site Ruins are located directly along the prehistoric trade routes on the Upper Little Colorado River Drainage. A long list of ceramic types are found on the site that were produced hundreds of miles away. These were traded into Raven

Site Ruins. Because of Raven Site Ruins' ideal trade location, abundant water, firewood, and several different colored clay sources for slips and clay bodies, the prehistoric peoples who occupied the site began to produce ceramics at an alarming rate. They produced this fine ceramic material to trade out. As they improved their ceramic technology, their trade with other regions increased. With each improvement in their ceramic technology, they increased their ability to trade these vessels to a wider market. By the year A.D. 1300, the potters at Raven Site Ruins were rapidly increasing their technological ability and expanding their markets. Between A.D. 1300 and A.D. 1380 over a dozen ceramic styles rapidly appeared. These ceramic types are the finest ever produced prehistorically in the White Mountains. This rapid development of new ceramic types and styles has been recently linked to the adoption of the Katsina Cult in the White Mountain area (Adams 91).

After A.D. 1380 these fine ceramics were no longer produced at the site. The north pueblo area was again all but abandoned and the potters who were producing these fine White Mountain Red Wares and Cibola White Wares moved north, probably to Homolovi near Winslow, Arizona. This is evident because this ceramic tradition continues at the Homolovi site. A new ceramic tradition continued at Raven Site Ruins using a vitreous glazing technique which gave birth to many new styles and designs. This new ceramic tradition continued at the site until approximately A.D. 1550. This new ceramic tradition evolved into the vitreous Zuni Glaze Wares, giving rise to several more ceramic types. Also, from A.D. 1380 to possibly as late as A.D.1550, new trade associations are evident. Ceramic types from the south began to appear with greater frequency.

The complexity of Raven Site Ruins ceramic assemblages will be discussed type by type, beginning with the earliest examples and moving through time to the latest so far discovered at the ruin. There are many styles that are unique to the site and are yet unnamed. Many of these ceramic styles are transitional occurring temporally between the appearance of one style and another. Prehistoric copies have also been discovered, these were produced at Raven Site Ruins but they are not a part of any of the ceramic traditions that evolved there. Many of these prehistoric copies are of a finer quality than the original types that they mimic.

Introduction

Raven Site Ruins, site number QR:11:48, is located in east/central Arizona, just 16 miles south of the town of St. Johns, Arizona and 12 miles north of Springerville (see map figure 1). It is the largest populational center along the Upper Little Colorado River Drainage. Eight miles south of the site is Hooper Ranch Pueblo with around 120 ground floor rooms. A few miles further south is the Casa Malpais ruin with approximately 40-60 rooms and a large square kiva. Three miles to the north of Raven Site is the location of the Lyman Lake Ruins. All along the river course populational centers can be found, but none are as large or were occupied as long as the Raven Site Ruins with over 800 rooms and a temporal depth from A.D. 800 through A.D. 1550.

The Raven Site Ruins complex consists of two pueblos, the north pueblo and the south pueblo. These two sections of the site appear to be distinct for several reasons. The north pueblo was occupied from as early as A.D. 800 through about A.D. 1380. The archaeologists working at the site are not sure if the site was occupied even earlier than A.D. 800. As the rooms in the north pueblo are excavated, every feature is stabilized and preserved for future study. A room will be excavated, and after a meter or two a floor will be discovered, complete with usually a central square hearth and other distinct floor features. All hearths are protected in order to obtain an archaeomagnetic date. The excavation then continues by creating an earthen column around the hearth and deeper grid cuts through the newly discovered floor. After perhaps another meter, another floor will be discovered with another hearth and other floor features from an even earlier occupation. This hearth and these floor features are stabilized and deep excavations continue. It is not uncommon to discover as many as ten distinct floor levels in a single three meter square area in the north pueblo. The original hill, i.e., the sterile gravel upon which the pueblo was built has not been discovered. This is because every place that has been excavated contains so many features, that it has not been possible, so far, to obtain the depth necessary to discover the original hill. It is very likely that pit houses could exist below the known features of the site. There are too many features in the way of discovering the original hill and possible original habitations of the site. The earliest date so far obtained is A.D. 800, but this is not to say that there are not even earlier occupations that pre-date A.D. 800.

Analysis of the north pueblo is wonderfully frustrating. Excavations will begin in a room, the four walls will be quickly discovered only a few centimeters below the surface of the site. The first few grids into the room will reveal that the room was filled with prehistoric trash. This indicates that the room was abandoned while neighboring rooms were still occupied. The prehistoric people would sweep up their hearth areas in the morning, climb up on the roof of their house, and throw the ash and animal bone into the abandoned room next door. Obviously the roof beams had to have been at least partially removed to accommodate this process. These trash middens contain abundant cultural material. People lose things in the trash. Points, beads, ear drops, ornaments, and other small objects are found. This trash will also contain all of the discarded tools and ceramic materials that were broken. Butchered animal bone and floral refuse are also layered in these cultural lenses. After the trash-filled room is excavated to the floor, previously existing rooms are found below the surface room. Often features from pre-existing rooms will be incorporated into the newer room above. Old foundations become benches or are used as small divider walls. In many places in the north pueblo there have been discovered rooms that were built on top of trash middens, and again, below the middens are earlier rooms.

The animal bone found in these rich trash middens reveals a wealth of information. What they ate, how they hunted, what animals they raised, differences in the prehistoric environment, seasonal variations of species and other information is disclosed. The north pueblo at the site has yielded hundreds of pounds of animal bone from the trash middens. The diversity of species discovered has been enormous. Ironically, the south pueblo has revealed very little faunal material. This is probably because we have not yet found the trash middens in the south pueblo, or, because the south pueblo inhabitants simply threw their trash into the abandoned rooms in the north pueblo and the faunal assemblage from the north pueblo simply represents both occupational locations. The problem with this second possibility is that we never find any of the later ceramic material from the south pueblo in the north pueblo trash. If the south pueblo peoples were dumping their trash in the abandoned rooms of the north pueblo, then we would expect to find their broken dishes along with the animal bones that they discarded.

Most of the faunal material from Raven Site Ruins demonstrates heavy butchering. The bone is stripped of meat, split open and the marrow sucked out. This is even true of the smaller game animals such as rabbits and small birds. These same bones were then boiled to remove the fat and other nutrients before they were discarded. This boiling process rounds the edges of the splintered bones. As the bones

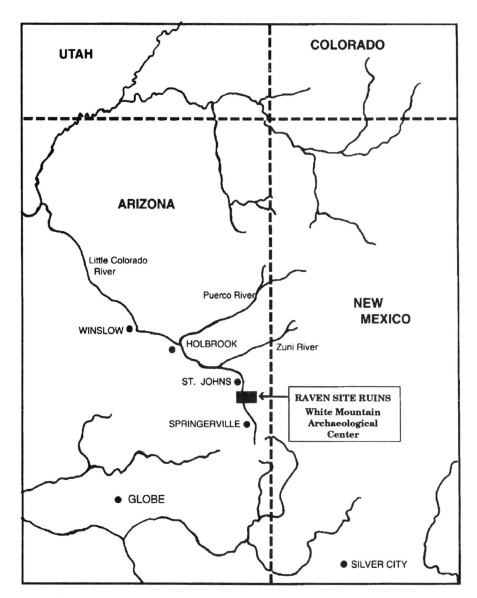

Figure 1. Location of Raven Site Ruins on the Little Colorado Plateau.

roll around in the boiling ceramic stew pot, they rub against the abrasive edges of the vessel and this rounds and smooths them. The later stages of this heavy butchering process has advantages and disadvantages to the modern archaeologist. Because the faunal material was boiled and the fat and collagen removed, these bones preserved in the middens fare better than they would have if they had not been boiled. There was little left in the bones to attract bacteria and rodents. However, because the collagen was removed by boiling, there is also little left in this faunal material to produce an accurate Carbon-14 date, unless a very large sample is utilized.

Artist's rendition of the South Pueblo at Raven Site Ruins, 1425 A.D.

Chapter 1

History Of Raven Site Ruins

Raven Site Ruins sits on a five acre knoll overlooking the Little Colorado River. Because of the site's close proximity to the river, the land upon which the site is located became private/patented land very early in Arizona's history. The pueblo was totally abandoned sometime after A.D. 1550 by the prehistoric inhabitants, and the room blocks and kivas silently fell into ruin over the next several centuries. The Athapaskan peoples, the Navajo and Apache, arrived in the Southwest around the same time as the Spanish conquistadors, i.e., A.D. 1540 (Cordell 84). The abandonment of Raven Site Ruins may have been at least partially because of this influx of enemies into the previously peaceful region. For many years these intruders preyed upon the Pueblo Indians. In A.D. 1680 the Indians of Zuni Pueblo rose in revolt against the Spanish and drove them from the area. Zuni Pueblo, where this history occurred, is less than one hundred miles north of Raven Site Ruins, and the principle route to Zuni Pueblo from the south passes within fifty meters of the site. The Spanish made repeated attempts to gain back their province. In A.D. 1692, Santa Fe Pueblo and several others were re-conquered by the Spanish, but much hard fighting followed. By A.D. 1695 peace was restored briefly, followed by another rebellion the following year (Grant 81).

In the years that followed, the Spanish governed the area of Raven Site Ruins and introduced sheep into the region. These sheepherders built homesteads of local rock and timbers. Just a few meters south of Raven Site Ruins there can be seen one of these Spanish sheepherder homesteads. This small stone building is constructed from rock that was removed from Raven Site Ruins. The beams in this Spanish structure may have also been removed from the prehistoric site. These beams will be cored and tested to see if they are indeed prehistoric. So far, good beam material has not yet been recovered from the south pueblo at Raven Site Ruins. It is possible that the beam material was removed by the early Spanish settlers and used elsewhere. The homestead just south of the site may contain the only remaining beam material that exists from the south pueblo. This lack of good tree-ring material from the south pueblo is frustrating. Other dating techniques are being utilized to help date the south pueblo at Raven Site Ruins, however, dendrochronology is by far the most accurate method known. The Zuni Glaze Ware ceramic types from the south pueblo have dates that have been assigned to each ceramic type in the sequence, however, there is an ongoing debate as to the accuracy of these dates. Good beam material would help verify when these pottery types were produced.

After A.D. 1860 the valley where Raven Site Ruins is located was homesteaded by the early Mormon settlers. The Sherwood family arrived in A.D. 1880 and re-developed the springs and irrigation systems that had been utilized by the prehistoric peoples of the site. The Sherwoods ranched in the valley, now called "Richiville" and they still raise cattle in the area to this day.

Around A.D. 1900 an Indian woman gained permission from the Sherwoods to loot the burials from Raven Site Ruins. Using Mexican and Navajo labor, she completely terraced the east slope outside the pueblo walls and removed thousands of pottery vessels. These vessels were sold to Santa Fe dealers and their whereabouts is now unknown. This same woman sold the skeletal material to Mexican witches. These were ground into potions. The absence of these burials is regrettable because of the loss of the scientific information that could have been obtained from their analysis, however, in today's political climate, it is advantageous not to have to encounter burials during modern excavations. After the initial looting of A.D. 1900, Raven Site Ruins remained undisturbed for many decades. In the early 1980s, modern looters using backhoes again gained permission to loot the site. Again the east slope outside the pueblo was systematically trenched with the hopes of finding commercially valuable cultural material. The modern looters with their diesel-powered scoops quickly discovered that the burials had already been removed. They then contented themselves by attempting to destroy the north pueblo and all of the scientific information it contained. They would approach a room with the backhoe, and scoop out the center, throwing earth, rock, ceramic, beads, points, and anything else in their way, aside. They would then scratch around briefly and move on to destroy another room. It was during this modern looting that the site was re-discovered by the scientific community. A bold archaeologist, being careful not to get shot, peeked into one of the scooped-out rooms. There he counted over fifty different ceramic types in a single looter's hole. This diversity of ceramics on a single site indicates a tremendous temporal depth. Realizing that Raven Site Ruins are an important and scientifically valuable part of Arizona's prehistory, efforts were then begun to save the site from further destruction.

Wendel and Ruth Sherwood, the owners of the land encompassing Raven Site Ruins, contacted every university in the Southwest in an attempt to have the site properly excavated and researched. None of these institutions expressed the means, manpower or interest to take on such an enormous project. They flatly rejected it. Ruth Sherwood took it upon herself to obtain some archaeological training in an attempt to excavate and curate the cultural material from the site. For many summers she excavated in the hot sun, her Boston terriers asleep under her screens. She recorded her information diligently, and catalogued the material she discovered. During the late 1980s The White Mountain Archaeological Center was formed with the sole purpose of preserving Raven Site Ruins and permanently curating the cultural material. Rather than rely upon spotty and often non-existent Federal and State money to accomplish this purpose, it was decided to create a system whereby anyone with an interest in archaeology could actually participate in the ongoing excavations and laboratory curation. Students from all over the world come to Raven Site Ruins to help excavate and curate the cultural material, and record the information.

About the White Mountain Archaeological Center

The White Mountain Archaeological Center is a nonprofit facility and was initially established to protect and preserve Raven Site Ruin. It has evolved into far more. The Center now not only directs the excavation and curation of the cultural material from the site, including all of the ceramics included in this book, but also offers hands-on archaeological excavation, lab work and survey to anyone with an interest in the archaeological sciences. The Center is open from April through October. Daily, multiple day and week-long programs are available. On-site lodging is available by reservation.

The on-site museum displays much of the cultural material discovered at Raven Site, and all of the artifacts are held in the repository at the same location. It is a rare opportunity to view all of the cultural material from a prehistoric pueblo in one place. Virtually all of the ceramic vessels illustrated in this book are on display at the Center, and they can be seen there seven days a week throughout the summer excavation season. Each year as the excavations continue, we eagerly await the cleaning and analysis in the lab, hoping that another Rosetta Stone similar to vessel SW1391a (Cunkle 93) will appear and give us more insights into the minds of the prehistoric potters who created these images.

If you would like to participate in the excavation or laboratory projects at the White Mountain Archaeological Center call or write to make reservations for your program. Your interest and excitement provides the means and the method for our continuing research.

If you have a prehistoric Southwest ceramic vessel, and this vessel exhibits what you believe to be coherent icons, or if you would like our staff to type and date the vessel, I would encourage you to send photographs of the pottery for possible translation and analysis. Our symbol dictionary is to date very small. The more vessels that can be translated, the larger our icon vocabulary will become, and there will be more that we will ultimately understand about the lives of the prehistoric peoples of the Southwest.

Author James R. Cunkle and staff

White Mountain Archaeological Center
H C 30
St. Johns, Arizona 85936
602-333-5857

Chapter 2

Site Features and Cultural Change

In the north pueblo there are at least five different masonry styles so far discovered. There are mud/cobble walls consisting of small rounded river cobbles embedded in a heavy mud mortar. These are very common in the extreme northeast area of the north pueblo. Elaborate banded basalt masonry consisting of large basalt rock in perfect linear rows surrounded by small chinking stones can be seen in the central north pueblo. Plain basalt dry laid masonry is found on the southwest corner of the north kiva. Plain red sandstone dry laid masonry can be see on the extreme western edge of the north pueblo. Also, a linear stacked wet laid travertine later intrudes into the north pueblo. This travertine masonry is the only masonry style in the south pueblo.

It is difficult to determine if there was ever a master plan for the origin of room blocks in the north pueblo. The eastern section appears to have been constructed first, but until further excavations are complete, and lower occupational levels are revealed, it will be impossible to tell if the north pueblo at any stage of construction was ever a planned community. This problem is further complicated by all of the additions and changes that occurred in the north pueblo. A fine banded wall will be discovered that had originally been an external wall of the pueblo. This wall was then used later as an internal wall and was plastered over as the pueblo expanded. There is one architectural feature in the north pueblo that appears to have been carefully planned and built. The extreme north point of the room blocks is terraced inward to the northernmost point of the hill. This gives this section a very MesoAmerican look. The outer wall zigzags in from as many as twelve rooms wide to a single room on the northernmost point of the site.

All of this evidence in the north pueblo indicates that there were several re-occupations of the site. There was a continual influx and exodus of population that lasted for several centuries. It is unlikely that the north pueblo was ever totally abandoned, until around A.D. 1380. Even the A.D. 1380 abandonment may not have been the total population.

Archaeologist Jeff Brown stabilizing a doorway. Room 31, South Pueblo, Raven Site Ruins.

Over 70 different ceramic types have been discovered at Raven Site Ruins including Cibola White Ware, White Mountain Red Ware and Zuni Glaze Ware.

About fifty meters south of the north pueblo is the south pueblo. This pueblo was built after A.D. 1380. This section of the site is very different from the north. All of the rooms exhibit the same masonry style, i. e., wet-laid stacked linear travertine. Most of the rooms that have been excavated to date have been almost exactly three meters square. Floors usually have central square, slab lined hearths, and these floors are polished cliche clay. These clay floors often will be blended into the walls. Small doorways are common from room to room. Rock lined ventilators for the fire draft are also common. There is very little evidence of any re-occupation of the south pueblo. No features below floor level had been discovered until the excavations during the 1993 field season. Usually in the south pueblo after a floor has been excavated, lower excavations reveal only the gravel of the original hill. In 1993, the archaeologists working in the south pueblo discovered mud gravel walls below the surface rooms, indicating that in at least some areas, there are earlier habitations below the surface features. The whole south pueblo was conceived and constructed along rigid guidelines. There are linear room blocks, eight rooms wide, oriented around a central kiva. This gives this pueblo a square horseshoe shape with a kiva in the middle. The south pueblo is very much a planned community. It was zoned. There was a master plan of construction, and it was probably entirely constructed in a short period of time.

The plaza on the site separates the north pueblo from the south pueblo. This plaza area was undoubtedly used by both communities. This brings us to a question yet unanswered at Raven Site Ruins. Even though the north pueblo is separate from the south pueblo by time and construction technique, the room blocks may actually connect from the north pueblo to the south pueblo. This has not yet been determined by excavation, and it is not possible to determine from surface features, with the exception of the extreme west room block of the south pueblo which does appear to connect with the kiva of the north pueblo. Furthermore, from the aerial photographs taken of the site, it appears that there is a perimeter wall that encompasses both pueblos. It may be that the south pueblo was built by the remaining inhabitants of the north pueblo after A.D. 1380 and that the entire site is a continuous habitational center.

Enclosing the central plaza during this time may be associated with the introduction of the Katsina Cult into the White Mountain area. Enclosed plazas to accommodate the viewing of the Katsina dancers are a site feature that is associated with the introduction of the Katsina Cult after A.D. 1300 (Adams 91).

Room 26, North Pueblo, Raven Site Ruins

Restoration, curation — Raven Site Ruins

There is also a continuation of a ceramic sequence from the ceramic material in the north pueblo to the ceramic sequence found in the south pueblo. The north pueblo potters produced fine Cibola White Wares and White Mountain Red Wares in a continuing sequence of pottery types beginning as early as A.D. 900 with Reserve Black-on-white and Puerco Red Ware. This sequence continues for several centuries and through dozens of types terminating with the Fourmile Polychrome pottery ending at A.D. 1380. However, around A.D. 1300, these potters re-discovered the use of copper and magnesium glazes. These glazes produce a beautiful glassy surface to the designs and colors include black, purple and even shiny greens. As beautiful as these glazes are, the prehistoric potters at Raven Site Ruins discovered a problem with their use. These glazes are very low-firing, and they will run during the firing process. The craftswoman would paint a detailed depiction on the interior of a bowl or on the exterior of a jar, only to have her fine brush lines run and drip together during the firing. One group of potters at Raven Site Ruins continued to use their traditional pigments, deciding that the new copper and magnesium glazes were too uncontrollable. They opted for the fine, controlled line work of the past. These potters continued with their traditional methods and produced the remaining White Mountain Red Ware sequence up to and including the Fourmile Polychromes of A.D. 1325 to A.D. 1380.

The other tradition that evolved began with the discovery of these new glazes around A.D. 1300. These potters liked the vitreous colors and continued to use them. This sequence begins with Heshotauthla Polychrome around A.D. 1300 and continues through a unique series of ceramic types that later become the Zuni Glaze Wares. The conclusion of this ceramic sequence at Raven Site Ruins ends with Matsaki Polychrome dating from A.D. 1475 to A.D. 1680. Heshotauthla Polychrome can be found in both the north and south pueblos at Raven Site Ruins. However, none of the other glaze wares in this later sequence are found in the north pueblo, they are found only in the south pueblo. This is to be expected, the north pueblo was abandoned by A.D. 1380, that is, before this ceramic sequence was full blown. In the south pueblo all of the ceramics discovered so far are glaze wares. As unique as both pueblos are with their distinct ceramic traditions, there is a continuation from the north pueblo to the south, because of the Heshotauthla Polychromes which begins this new ceramic sequence that continues in the south pueblo with its later occupational dates.

Chapter 3

Functional Versus Ceremonial

When a single object is recovered from a prehistoric site, the analysis of that object is often only speculative. If only one object of a particular form is found, too often the archaeological community will abandon further analysis of that artifact, classify its form and function all too briefly then throw it into the taxonomical black hole of "ceremonial". This is not good science. Any artifact in isolation says very little. For example, if the scientific community, to date, had only a single shaft abrader in all of the collections of Southwest cultural material, that lonely tool would undoubtedly be typed as a ceremonial object instead of a utilitarian object, as is its true function. One could argue that common objects, tools, utensils, are commonly found; and that esoteric, ceremonial, and sacred objects are unique and rarely discovered. This is true to some extent, however, we cannot ignore the demon of preservation and the possibility that true ceremonial objects were manuported off the site during the frequent migrations. When a prehistoric site is excavated, only a tiny fraction of the total cultural assemblage is ever recovered. We find some flint, bone, ceramic and occasional bit of fabric. These prehistoric peoples had every bit as complex of a culture as any other human group. They traded objects from MesoAmerica to Canada. They carried live Macaw parrots from the jungles of Central America to the snow-covered mountains of the far North. Shells from the Gulf of California are found as far east as Ohio. They had marriage customs, trade associations, songs, poems, language and a social system as complex as ours is today. They laughed and cried and cared for one another as much and as little as all human animals do. The fragmentary smattering of the remains of their culture that we are fortunate enough to excavate today, are but a peek into their past.

When the archaeologist is fortunate enough to discover a persevered piece of a pre-existing culture, and his/her discovery is the first of its kind, to lump that previously unseen object into the muddy category of "ceremonial" is scientifically negligent.

When you examine the collections from any archaeological site, you will see dozens of shaft abraders, hammers, loom weights, metates, monos, bone tools, points, saws, drills, pottery anvils, mortars, pestles, and yes, a few objects that might have a ceremonial significance, but that "ceremonial" significance/function must be downplayed against the overwhelming evidence of utilitarian possibilities.

99.999% of humankind's day-to-day activities and consequentially remains/artifacts, are utilitarian. The bulk of the artifacts from Raven Site Ruins are indeed common, everyday items that were used, traded, broken, re-worked and later discarded. When you encounter in the academic literature an artifact that has been classified as "ceremonial" a caution flag should pop up in your mind. That classification is often an indication that the researcher has no clue to the artifact's true function. I can imagine a confused archaeologist in the far future excavating the first Coors® beer can ever found, and displaying it in the museum as a ceremonial object.

As the layers of the past are stripped away, and many similar artifacts of form and function are recovered, it is then far easier to discern the true nature and use of the pieces. One hundred similar artifacts can reveal more of the prehistoric culture than can the splashy discovery of the cache of a kiva vault with one or two unique artifacts. When you view the artifacts from any Southwest cultural group, and look at the assemblage of shaft abraders, or axes, or hammers, you will notice that these tools are different sizes, they are made out of several different types of stone, they have different hafting characteristics (in the case of tools that had handles) and they are each both unique and yet similar because of their function. I am reminded of the contents of my screwdriver drawer. That drawer contains dozens of different sizes of the same tool. They have different handles, different markings on the handles and shafts, different lengths of shafts and sizes of tips. And yet, they are all necessary for my day-to-day function around this ranch and archaeological site.

Chapter 4

The White Mountain Red Wares of Raven Site Ruins

This is the first sequence of ceramics that we will examine from Raven Site Ruins, which begins with the production of Puerco Black-on-red around the year A.D. 900 and continues through a variety of types and then terminates with the Fourmile Polychrome ceramics which were produced until around A.D. 1400. This series of ceramic types has a temporal development over 500 years long.

PUERCO BLACK-ON-RED

DATES — Puerco Black-on-red pottery was produced between the years A.D. 1000 and continued through A.D. 1200. This two hundred years of production overlaps several other ceramic styles and types that are very similar and often difficult to differentiate from Puerco Black-on-red. Many vessels that have been typed as Puerco Black-on-red may actually be early versions of other, later ceramics that continue the series. This is a problem that we will encounter throughout the White Mountain Red Ware series. If the vessels have only a red slip and the addition of black paint, i.e.,. no other colors, it is often very difficult to type the vessels accurately. There are other type indicators that we will utilize, such as style, form, and design units, but one must keep in mind that these ceramics are evolving, changing into other types slowly over time. This means that a late Puerco Black-on-red will very much resemble an early Wingate Black-on-red, that is, the next ceramic type in the series. This evolution can best be demonstrated with the various widths of white paint on the exterior of St. Johns Polychrome bowls (see St. Johns Polychrome).

CONSTRUCTION — Puerco Black-on-red vessels are constructed using the coil and scrape method and are slipped red on the interior and exterior of bowls, and on the exterior of jars. Occasionally, in the case of jars, this slip will continue into the neck of the jar. This treatment is not uncommon with many of the ceramics that we will examine.

The paste or body of the clay ranges in color from light brown to orange, rarely white to grey. The black paint is iron and sometimes an iron/carbon mixture and it does penetrate the slip.

The polish on these vessels varies. In the case of bowls the interior is better polished, that is, smoother than the exterior in many instances.

On the exterior of bowls, the temper particles often protrude through the slip. This indicates that the slip is thin and poorly executed. Remember the exterior of Puerco Black-on-red bowls are not decorated with designs, only the red slip color. The design field is the interior of the bowl. This interior is the canvas where the artist creates her designs, and it is necessary to execute a smooth, more finished surface for this purpose. Many of the ceramic types in the Southwest that share a production date around the year A.D. 1000 utilize only the interior of the bowl for painted design elements, and in most cases the ceramic bowls of this period exhibit crudely polished exteriors. The best examples are the Mimbres vessels found to the south and east of Raven Site Ruins with their wonderful interior designs, and unfinished, crude exteriors.

The slip thickness on Puerco Black-on-red varies and it often appears weathered. Fire clouds on the exterior of bowls are common.

FORM — The collections from Raven Site Ruins contain only three examples of Puerco Black-on-red, other than sherds, which exhibit vessel form—one small dipper and two bowls. The dipper is crude, with poor clay construction, although the slip is rather thick. The two bowls are the classic Puerco form with rounded bottoms and vertical sides. Bowls normally have no inward edge curvature this early in the White Mountain Red Ware series.

Photo 1. Puerco Black-on-red bowl and dipper from Raven Site Ruins.
This ceramic style was produced between A.D. 1000 and A.D. 1200 and is the first type in the White Mountain Red Ware series. The black paint is found only on the interior of bowls and on the exterior of jars. No white paint is utilized.

PAINTED/DECORATIONS/DESIGNS— Bowl interiors are painted with black designs usually in the typical Puerco Style, Holbrook Style, and very late examples will often exhibit a Wingate Style. The area at the bottom of the bowl is usually left undecorated and defined by a circle. Banding lines are sometimes present on the upper edge of the rim, and they are usually the same width as the hachuring and frets. Hachuring is rarely utilized. The classic Puerco Style exhibits simple triangular or square spirals as seen on the dipper and bowl in Photo 1. They are produced with lines that are usually of the same width, with a symmetrical design scheme.

DISTRIBUTION — Raven Site Ruins is not the core area for the spacial distribution of Puerco Black-on-red. The core area is to the north and slightly east of the site on both sides of the New Mexico/Arizona state line (see map, Fig 2, page 15).

REMARKS — Puerco Black-on-red is the first ceramic type in the White Mountain Red Ware sequence. The vessels are painted red on the interior and exterior, jars on the exterior, with simple black painted designs on the interior only of bowls and the exterior of jars. There are only the two colors present.

As the White Mountain Red Ware sequence continues, we will see that the introduction of white kaolin paint in addition to the black paint on a red slipped surface, is instrumental in ceramic type differentiation. With the future addition of the white paint, three colors will be utilized. The red slip is included as a color. The black, white, and red vessels are called polychromes. Puerco Black-on-red is not a polychrome, there is never a white paint present on a Puerco Black-on-red vessel, and no Puerco Polychromes exist to date. As we proceed through the White Mountain Red Ware series, we will discover that the addition of the white paint greatly aids in type classification for the polychrome vessels. However, for the next few hundred years polychromes are produced side by side with vessels that exhibit only two colors, the red slip and the black paint. These Black-on-red vessels are very often difficult to accurately type. To further confuse the classification, most of these ceramic types overlap temporally. These problems will be addressed as the photographic examples are shown.

WINGATE BLACK-ON-RED

DATES — A.D. 1050 to A.D. 1200 (Carlson 70). Wingate Black-on-red was produced just before the northern Anasazi peoples abandoned the San Juan area, including Chaco. This ceramic type also temporally directly overlays Puerco Black-on-red.

CONSTRUCTION — Vessels are constructed using the coil and

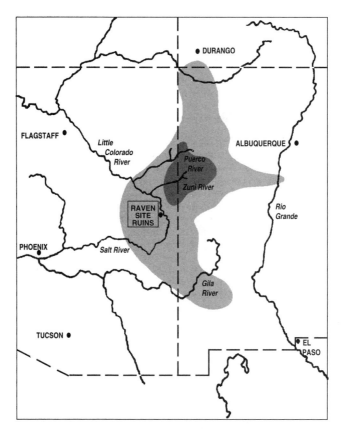

Figure 2. Distribution of Puerco Black-on-red. *The core area where this ceramic type was produced is just north and east of Raven Site Ruins. This could indicate that the early settlers at Raven Site Ruins arrived from just north of the site around the year A.D. 1000. (From Carlson 70)*

scrape method. Bowls and dippers are heavily slipped on the interior and exterior surfaces in red. Jars are slipped on the exterior and this red coloring will often continue into the neck of the jar. This slip is polished into the clay on all surfaces, however, this polishing is often not well smoothed.

The body of the clay can be white to grey, it sometimes even appears pink. The clay temper is usually sherd fragments. The black paint is an iron and carbon mixture (Hawley 50) and it can range from a light brown to a good black.

FORM — Bowls have rounded bottoms, with rims that are often flattened at the top edge. There is no inward curvature of the rim of bowls.

PAINTED/DECORATION/DESIGN — Bowls are slipped red on the interior and exterior with painted black designs only on the interior.

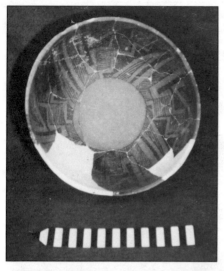

2a

Photo 2a & 2b. Wingate Black-on-red bowl *showing the often fuzzy edges of the black paint on the bowl interior. The bottom of the bowl is banded by a circle and left undecorated. On the exterior of this bowl is a small isolated "signature" design element in black.*

2b

Occasionally a small isolated design element in the same black paint can be discovered on the exterior of bowls. This could be called a signature element or ownership mark (Roberts 32). Jars are painted black on red on the exterior. Vessels are normally decorated in a classic Wingate Style, although later in the temporal span of this ceramic type, some vessels appear that are decorated in the Tularosa Style. These are very difficult to differentiate from St. Johns Black-on-red vessels, i.e., temporally the next ceramic type in the sequence of White Mountain Red Wares.

With Wingate Black-on-red vessels, the hachuring design elements begin to predominate the design field. These are combined with interlocked elements in solid black paint. The solid units are usually narrower than the hachured units. These hachured and solid design elements are usually separated by an unpainted area in between. Fields of design are usually symmetrical.

DISTRIBUTION — The spacial distribution of Wingate Black-on-red is shown in Figure 3. Raven Site Ruins is just south and west of the core area, as in the case with Puerco Black-on-red. Wingate Black-on-red has a much wider distribution in all directions than does Puerco Black-on-red. The appearance of Wingate Black-on-red decreases rapidly west of the Little Colorado River, that is, west of Raven Site Ruins.

REMARKS — We have now introduced Puerco Black-on-red and Wingate Black-on-red. Both types were produced at the same time and in nearly the same areas. Both types use only a black paint on a red slipped surface to create their designs. The best way to distinguish between the two ceramic types is to compare the design elements and execution. Puerco Black-on-red uses very little hachuring, the designs

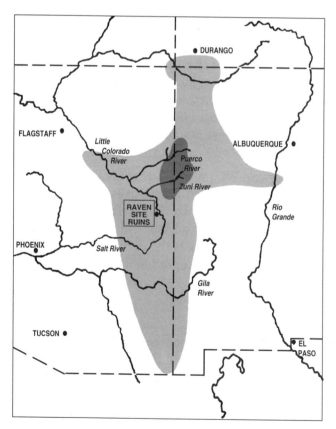

*Figure 3. **Wingate Black-on-red area of distribution and greatest concentration.** Wingate Black-on-red has a much wider range than does Puerco Black-on-red. (From Carlson 70)*

are focused around the center of the bowl, and solid symmetrical units predominate. Wingate Black-on-red uses much more hachuring interlocked with smaller solid black units and there is an unpainted area between the two. The transition in style that we are witnessing by making this comparison, is the temporal change from the use of the Puerco and Holbrook "styles" to the Wingate and slightly later the Tularosa "styles". (If you are totally confused at this point, refer to *Ceramic Styles of the White Mountains,* page 115).

WINGATE POLYCHROME

DATES — A.D. 1125 to A.D. 1200 and some varieties exhibiting the Tularosa Style may have been produced as late as A.D. 1300 (Carlson 70).

CONSTRUCTION — Vessels are constructed using the coil and scrape method. The body of the clay is usually light-colored and ranges from brown to orange or buff. The temper of the clay is sometimes sherd. Quartz particles are often present.

The black paint ranges from dull brown to a good black and is composed of copper, iron/carbon, and manganese (Colton/Hargrave 37). The white paint is kaolin. The addition of this white paint primarily on the exterior of bowls introduces the third color. Occasionally this white paint will outline the designs on the interior of bowls, although no examples exhibiting this treatment have been discovered to date at Raven Site Ruins. The red slip, black painted interior designs, and now primarily white exterior designs result in the first polychrome vessel in the White Mountain Red Ware series.

The use of slip colors on Wingate Polychromes and their application is interesting. Bowl exteriors exhibit no overall slip, but instead wide designs in red slip are applied to the surface of an orange/brown or white clay. White slip is then added and polished between the red. Another treatment with the slip is the reverse. The bowl exteriors are slipped with white paint and then wide designs are created over this using a red slip paint.

The key to recognizing a Wingate Polychrome vessel as opposed to later polychrome ceramic types is the presence of these wide exterior designs in both red and white slip. Remember, the interior of bowls is usually painted with just black-on-red, and these interior bowl designs can be frustratingly similar to Puerco Black-on-red, and later, St. Johns Black-on-red, the next ceramic type in the series.

FORM — Bowls have rounded bases. The rim of these can be vertical, but inward curving is sometimes present. The top of the rim now begins to demonstrate variation. Some rims are rounded, other examples show a deliberate flattening. Some bowls have an internal

Photo 3a & 3b. Wingate Polychrome bowl, a, interior and b, exterior. *The execution quality and width of the exterior white/red designs are a key to determining if the vessel is an early Wingate Polychrome or one that was produced later in the temporal span. The width and execution of exterior white lines as a dating aid will also be discussed with many later ceramic types in the White Mountain Red Ware series.*

3b

bevel on the rim and/or an external lip around the top of the bowl.

PAINTED DESIGNS — Bowl interiors are usually painted only in black on a thick red slip. Bowl exteriors are painted with wide designs in both red and cream/white kaolin paint. These wide white and red designs are usually simple, and in the earlier vessels rather crude, appearing almost like "finger painting". Wide bands of white will circle the exterior of the bowl, or a single simple star-shaped pattern will cover the bottom of the bowl. The earlier examples of Wingate Polychrome usually have wider and simpler exterior white/red designs. The later Wingate Polychromes show a marked improvement in the execution of these exterior designs and the line work becomes

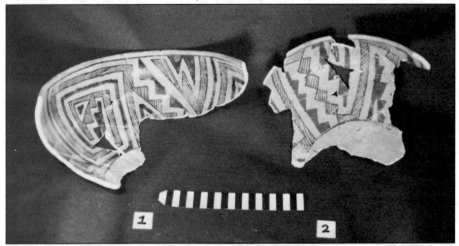

Photo 3c. Wingate Polychrome bowl glue-up sections, interior.

*Photo 3d. **Wingate Polychrome bowl sections** from photo 3c, showing exterior with wide white slip designs.*

narrower and better executed. By recognizing the width of the white designs on the exterior of Wingate Polychrome bowls, and the quality of their execution, it is possible in a very general way to recognize an early Wingate Polychrome from a later one. We will encounter this progression of quality of execution and line width again when we examine the St. Johns Polychromes, that is, the next ceramic type in the White Mountain Red Ware sequence. Often these white/red exterior designs include hand prints, bird feet, very simple scrolls, and simple interlocked designs.

On the interior of bowls the designs are created using black paint. The hachured units are still somewhat wider than the solid black units and

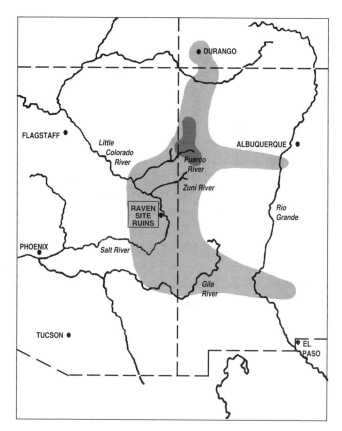

Figure 4. Distribution of Wingate Polychrome. *This ceramic type shares the basic core areas of Puerco Black-on-red and Wingate Black-on-red distribution, however, this new polychrome from the White Mountains appears to have been traded to the north and south (From Carlson 70).*

there remains an unpainted space between the solid and hachured unit, the same as Wingate Black-on-red. These designs are almost always symmetrical. The design styles that can be found on the interior of bowls run the gamut of Puerco Style and Holbrook Style in early examples, to Wingate Style and finally Tularosa Style on vessels that were produced later during the production of this ceramic type.

DISTRIBUTION — Wingate Polychrome can be found as far north as Durango and as far south as the Gila River (see Figure 4), although the distribution is primarily the same as Puerco Black-on-red and Wingate Black-on-red. Because Wingate Polychrome is the first polychrome that was produced in the White Mountains, a thin, but wider north-to-south distribution should be expected along the pochteca trade routes, as these new vibrant vessels were exchanged.

REMARKS — Several good examples of Wingate Polychrome have been excavated at Raven Site Ruins. Only one whole bowl has so far been discovered, but several vessels are emerging sherd by sherd from the disturbed areas of the north pueblo. What is interesting about this ceramic type, is the experimentation that the prehistoric potters were attempting with slips and exterior designs. With these experiments the first polychrome pottery from the White Mountains is invented. These first attempts at producing a polychrome pottery may have been stimulated by tradewares from the north, where polychrome pottery had existed earlier in the Kayenta area. The results of these early attempts to produce a high quality polychrome pottery were successful and the next type in this series, i.e., the St. Johns Polychrome ceramics, were widely traded and highly valued. They were also abundantly produced at Raven Site Ruins. Diagnostically, the difference between the Wingate Polychromes and the St. Johns Polychromes is that the St. Johns Polychromes have an overall exterior red slip and then white kaolin paint is added over this slip. The white exterior painted designs on St. Johns Polychrome vessels are thinner-lined than the Wingate Polychromes, and the Wingate Polychrome potters are using various slips and slip applications to produce the white and red exterior designs.

ST. JOHNS BLACK-ON-RED

DATES — A.D. 1175 to around A.D. 1300. These dates are the same as for St. Johns Polychrome vessels. St. Johns Black-on-red and polychrome vessels slightly overlap temporally with Wingate Polychrome ceramic production in the White Mountains of Arizona. The St. Johns vessels are a definitive development from the earlier Wingate ceramics.

CONSTRUCTION — Vessels are constructed using the coil and scrap method. The paste or body of the clay is now white to grey in most cases. This seems to indicate a high firing temperature. Occasionally in the White Mountain Archaeological Collections from Raven Site Ruins, a low-fired vessel of the St. Johns variety is found. These lower fired vessels exhibit the same paste/clay body color as the earlier Wingate ceramic types. This change in paste coloration, i.e., from the earlier brown to orange to buff to the advanced grey to white, could simply be the development of better firing techniques. The temper used in the clay now is almost always sherd temper, another advancement. The paint is iron/carbon and in the earlier vessels it has a fuzzy appearance. The later St. Johns Polychromes have a black paint that is sharp and defined. This is largely due to a technological development around A.D. 1300, i.e., the development of a vitreous glaze paint using increased copper and manganese minerals. This development results in a split ceramic tradition at Raven Site Ruins which continues side by side on the site (see *Zuni Glaze Wares,* page 58).

The slip found on St. Johns Black-on-red vessels is red both on the interior and exterior of bowls and on the exterior of jars. There is a tremendous variation in slip color after firing. The intended color was always a true red, however, there seems to be a lot of experimentation happening. At Raven Site Ruins, vessels are found that appear brown, orange, and others that are brilliant red. This variation appears to be caused by low firing, the brown and off-red colors resulting from under-firing and the bright reds resulting from high firing temperatures. This is the same problem that we have observed with the clay bodies. The white to grey are a high-fired body, and the orange, brown, or buff clay bodies are low-fired.

Sufficient specimens from Raven Site Ruins are contained in the White Mountain Archaeological Centers collections to conduct experimental re-firings on several presumed low-fired sherds. These experiments will resolve this issue. If re-firing of these presumed low-fired sherds results in a grey to white clay body and a brilliant red, then low firing was the culprit resulting in these color variations.

FORM — Bowls are usually deep, with rounded sides and bottoms. Often rims of bowls are in-curved. External lips on bowls are often present. No examples of St. Johns Black-on-red jars have been discovered to date at Raven Site Ruins, however, as of the year 1993, only 22 rooms have been excavated out of a total of 800. More examples

Photo 4a and 4b. St. Johns Black-on-red bowls. No painted designs appear on the exterior of these vessels. The interior of these bowls usually exhibit open bottoms and either Wingate, and more usually Tularosa Style, designs which often include the interlocked spiral units.

Photo 4c. Large sherds of St. Johns Black-on-Red. *The hachured units are still slightly larger than the solid units, but the hachured units are usually smaller than those found on Wingate vessels. This is typical of Tularosa Style.*

will undoubtedly emerge as excavations continue.

PAINTED DESIGNS — Bowls are black on red on the interior and red slip only on the exterior. Jars are black on red. Usually the bottom of bowls is left undecorated and banded by a circle. The hachured units are often still slightly larger than the solid unit, but often they are nearly equivalent. The unpainted red areas are still present between the hachured and solid interlocked units. All of the styles that we have so far encountered, that is, Puerco, Holbrook, Wingate, and Tularosa, can be found exhibited on St. Johns Black-on-red vessels. However, the predominant style of design is Tularosa, with hachured spirals interlocked with solid spirals and an area of red left unpainted in between.

DISTRIBUTION — As with most of the research that has so far been conducted concerning the White Mountain Red Ware sequence of pottery development, the core area of production of St. Johns Black-on-red has previously been determined to be north and east of Raven Site Ruins. As the excavations at Raven Site Ruins continue and as literally tons of ceramic material are unearthed from the site, these core areas of production will undoubtedly shift south and west.

REMARKS — St. Johns Black-on-red is an identical pottery to St. Johns Polychrome except that it lacks the addition of white paint on the exterior of bowls. It is often difficult to distinguish between St. Johns Black-on-red and Wingate Black-on-red, in fact, many vessels are not possible to accurately "split" into one type or the other. This is because ceramic development happens gradually over time. Changes occur slowly and types overlap. Carlson reports that it is often difficult to

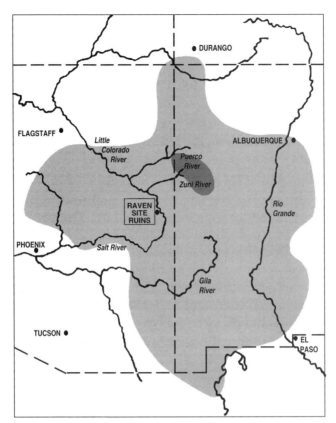

Figure 5. Core area of the production of St. Johns Black-on-red. *Many of these White Mountain Red Wares have previously been reported as having a core production area to the north and east of Raven Site Ruins. However, as excavations continue, and tons of ceramic materials are discovered, these areas of production may shift south and west. (From Carlson 70)*

distinguish between St. Johns Black-on-red and Pinto Black-on-red (Carlson 70). With the ceramic material contained in the White Mountain Archaeological Centers collections from Raven Site Ruins, these two ceramic types are easily distinguished by paste and slip. This is largely due to the fact that the St. Johns Black-on-reds found at Raven Site Ruins were produced at the same location, whereas the Pinto Black-on-red examples were traded in from below the Mogollon Rim. When vessels are produced in different locations the differences, especially when they are in fact different types, are more obvious.

ST. JOHNS POLYCHROME

DATES — St. Johns Polychrome was produced from A.D. 1175 to A.D. 1300. This type overlaps with Wingate Polychrome in the earlier phases of production and the two types are often very difficult to differentiate. The later St. Johns Polychromes overlap with another ceramic type named Heshotauthla. This new type which appears around the year A.D. 1300, will begin our discussion of the Zuni Glaze Wares (see *Zuni Glaze Wares,* page 58). This new ceramic type is the result of new glaze ware technologies and it is very distinct and easily recognizable.

CONSTRUCTION — Vessels are produced using the coil and scrape method. The body of the clay runs the gamut of color from white to grey, buff, pink, and we now occasionally see a black. This black paste could be the result of high firing and the use of a scoria or volcanic temper.

The white paint on the exterior of bowls is kaolin. It is thin, chalky, and it is often very faded from poor preservation. The black paint ranges from a faded brown to a shiny glaze black. Usually the earlier St. Johns Polychromes will exhibit the duller, brownish paint. This early black paint is primarily iron (Kidder/Shepard 36). The vessels produced later will have the vitreous black. This is largely due to the development of this glaze paint around A.D. 1300. The glaze paint has higher concentrations of manganese and copper.

Red slip covers both the interior and exterior of bowls and the exterior of jars. Occasionally a white slip is used in combination with the red, although no examples of this application have been discovered at Raven Site Ruins.

FORM — Bowls are rounded and deep with rims that are often slightly in-curved. The edge of the bowls rarely taper, they usually bevel and will often have an external lip. Jars are rare.

PAINTED DESIGNS — Carlson reports that several of the bowls

Photo 5a & 5b. St. Johns Polychrome bowl. The exterior white paint is the key to distinguishing St. Johns Polychrome from Wingate Polychrome. The white designs are narrower than Wingate. These white designs seem to have become even narrower and better executed later in the production of this type. The interior of this bowl is very unusual in that it displays an anthromorph (see Symbols, page 139).

that he examined used white paint on the interior to outline black motifs (Carlson 70). No examples of this interior white paint have been discovered at Raven Site Ruins. St. Johns Polychrome bowls are usually slipped in red on the interior and exterior, and jars on the exterior.

On bowls the exterior is decorated with white kaolin paint on the red slip. These white designs circle the exterior of the bowl below the rim and well onto the body of the vessel. They usually continue around the entire bowl and are only rarely broken into units. The line width of this white exterior paint varies from a fine thin line to a wide and poorly executed line that is often difficult to differentiate from the earlier Wingate Polychromes. There may be a development from the wider white exterior motifs to a finer, thinner execution as the type develops over time. This is substantiated by the next ceramic types in the sequence, which exhibit finer line work, and by the ceramic tradition "split" of the White Mountain Red Wares and the Zuni Glaze Wares around A.D. 1300. The Zuni Glaze Wares exhibit a very fine, beautifully executed exterior white line, in the case of bowls.

Usually bowls have a black on red interior and a white on red exterior. Tularosa Style designs are most common on bowl interiors with interlocked units, hachured and solid with an unpainted area between. Bowl bottoms are usually left undecorated.

DISTRIBUTION — St. Johns Polychrome has a very wide distribution and can be found as far south as Mexico, north into Colorado, west of Flagstaff, Arizona and as far east as Texas. The core area of production is believed to be just north and east of Raven Site Ruins in east/central New Mexico. Gladwin and Gladwin consider the production center to be within a fifty-mile radius of St. Johns, Arizona (Gladwin/Gladwin 31).

REMARKS — St. Johns Polychrome is a turning point in the ceramics that were produced at Raven Site Ruins. This type was produced in tremendous quantities and was undoubtedly an important trade item prehistorically. This is demonstrated by its wide distribution, and by the tons of sherds that have been excavated at the site. Ceramic production increased sharply just before A.D. 1300 at Raven Site Ruins, and this increased production continued for several decades.

With this increase in trade, coupled by the new glaze ware technologies that were discovered, the Raven Site potters began to explore many ceramic possibilities, including new colors, new slips, and new forms. A.D. 1300 ends the St. Johns Polychrome ceramic production and begins a duality of ceramic tradition at Raven Site Ruins. The White

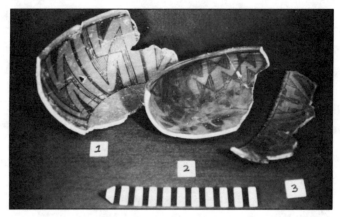

Photo 5c. Large sections of St. Johns Polychrome bowls, *interior. Hachuring is usually larger than the solid black areas, which is common with the Tularosa Style.*

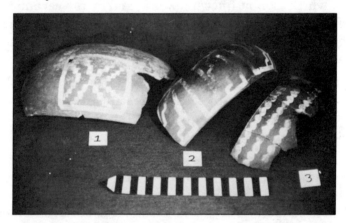

Photo 5d. Large bowl sections of St. Johns Polychrome *showing the exterior of those shown in Photo 5c.*

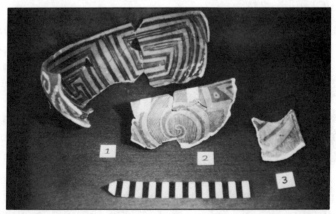

Photo 5e. St. Johns Polychrome bowl sections *showing interior designs. The interlocked spiral is a common motif.*

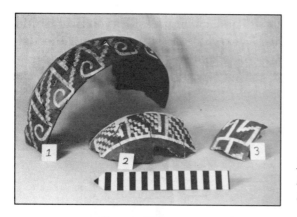

Photo 5f. The exterior of St. Johns Polychrome bowls *shown in Photo 5e.*

Photo 5g. St. Johns Polychrome bowl sections *showing interior. Example 1 uses a glaze paint which is very vitreous and common in later types (see Zuni Glaze Wares, page 58).*

Photo 5h. St. Johns Polychromes. *The exterior of the examples shown in 5g*

Mountain Red Ware ceramic tradition continues at Raven Site Ruins, with the introduction of several vessel types which we will discuss. Another contemporaneous group of potters at the site, began to produce ceramics that follow an entirely different direction, i.e., the Zuni Glaze Wares.

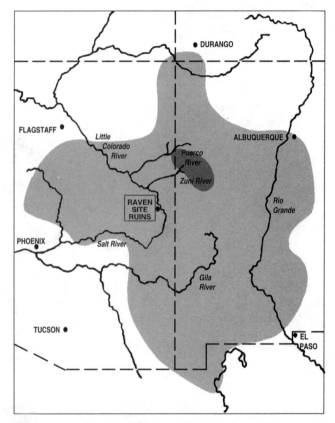

Figure 6. Distribution of St. Johns Polychrome. *This is essentially the same area as St. Johns Black-on-red. St. Johns Polychrome was widely traded. (From Carlson 70)*

SPRINGERVILLE POLYCHROME

DATES — Springerville Polychrome was produced in a very small core area between A.D. 1250 and A.D. 1300. These dates were obtained using the Maverick Mountain Phase at Point of Pines Ruin (Haury 58) and for the moment seem to be the most reliable. As the excavations continue at Raven Site Ruins, better dates may be possible because Raven Site Ruins is located in the center core area for the production of this ceramic type, and the overall range of this type is minimal.

CONSTRUCTION — Vessels are produced using the coil and scrape method. The body of the clay is grey, white and often buff, and the temper in almost all cases appears to be ground sherds.

The slip color is predominantly orange rather than red. This color variation is instrumental in the differentiation of many "black-on-red" and polychrome ceramic types. The orange rather than a red slip is a flag that often helps distinguish one type from another. The black paint can be either dull brown or true black. It seems to penetrate the slip. The white paint is kaolin and, as with the other ceramic types of this temporal period, it is chalky and sometimes suffers the ravages of preservation.

FORM — Bowls are not as deep in most cases as St. Johns vessels. The rims do have a similar in-curvature. Rims of bowls are rounded, sometimes beveled, and they sometimes have an external lip.

PAINTED DESIGNS — The first thing to remember about the identification of Springerville Polychrome, is that it is identical to St. Johns Polychrome *except* that there is black paint in addition to the white painted exterior designs. Don't forget that the slip is often orange rather than a true red.

A.D. 1300 is a pivotal point in time with relation to the White Mountain Red Wares. There is a lot of experimentation going on. This is because the prehistoric people recognized the value of a good trade network. They were

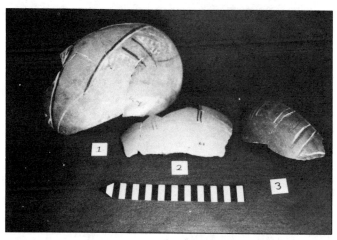

Photo 6. Springerville Polychrome bowl fragments, exterior. *This ceramic type is rare even in the core area of production. Designating Springerville Polychrome as a distinct type may be erroneous. These may simply be a variation of St. Johns Polychrome. However, by "splitting" these variations as a specific type, this enhances the ceramicist's ability to assign a date to these variations. Example 1 in this photo is probably a Heshotauthla Polychrome with the addition of black paint on the exterior.*

trying to produce better, more marketable ceramic styles and colors.

Bowls are painted in black on red (orange) on the interior and black/ white/ on red (orange) on the exterior. No examples of jars have yet been discovered from Raven Site Ruins. Even bowls are rare. White always predominates over black on bowl exteriors.

Design motifs are identical to St. Johns Polychromes, interior and exterior for bowls, and exterior for jars. The addition of a few strokes of black paint on the exterior of bowls is the only difference between a St. Johns Polychrome and a Springerville Polychrome vessel.

DISTRIBUTION — The core area of Springerville Polychrome centers directly upon Raven Site Ruins (Carlson 70). However, few distinct examples exist even in the White Mountain Archaeological

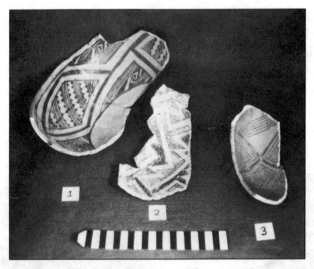

Photo 6a. Springerville Polychromes. These are the interior of the large bowl sections shown in Photo 6. Example 1 is probably a Heshotauthla Polychrome with vitreous interior paint.

Centers Collections. This could be because we have excavated only a fragment of the site. It is more likely that the type is simply a variant of St. Johns Polychrome, and Springerville Polychrome may well pass by the wayside along with Whipple Black-on-white and other ceramic "types" that were named and entered in the taxonomy.

REMARKS — Springerville Polychrome can best be defined as a variant of St. Johns Polychrome. The two types are identical except that Springerville Polychrome has a few strokes of black paint on the exterior of bowls, and the slip is often more orange than red. Springerville Polychrome is undoubtedly a late variation of St. Johns Polychrome.

This use of the exterior black paint in conjunction with the white continues to be found on another ceramic type which follows temporally, i.e., Heshotauthla. Heshotauthla is the first in our series of Zuni Glaze Wares which begins around A.D. 1300 (see Zuni Glaze Wares).

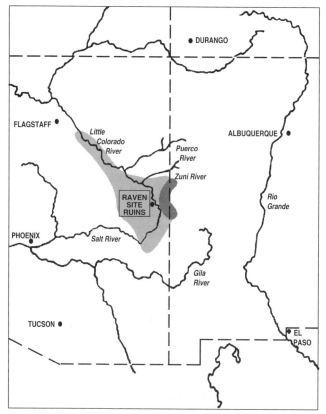

Figure 7. Distribution of Springerville Polychrome
(From Carlson 70)

PINEDALE BLACK-ON-RED

DATES — Pinedale Black-on-red shares a common temporal span with Pinedale Polychrome. This ceramic type was produced between A.D. 1275 to A.D. 1325. The ceramics of the White Mountains change dramatically after the year A.D. 1300. This is largely due to an increase in ceramic production as trade items. This was further stimulated by new ceramic technologies.

CONSTRUCTION — Pinedale Black-on-red vessels were constructed using the coil and scrape method. The body of the clay is buff or red/brown, and occasionally grey. The temper is usually ground sherds, and occasionally sand.

The slip color of these vessels in the White Mountain Archaeological Centers Collections are all very orange, although Carlson reports that a true red, as is found on Pinedale Polychromes, is more frequent (Carlson 70). Bowls are slipped red or orange on the interior and exterior and jars on the exterior.

The black paint on these vessels demonstrates the changes that were occurring during this time. The paint can be matte, but it ranges from matte to a shiny glaze black. These glaze paints have a high concentration of copper and manganese.

FORM — Bowls are globular, medium depth, and have in-curved rims. An external lip is sometimes present. Jars are globular with vertical necks, and often animal effigy lugs are used.

PAINTED DESIGNS — Pinedale vessels use very unit, singular designs on the exteriors. These almost appear to be signature elements in some cases. Others of these units are repeated around the exterior of the vessel, but they are never connected by any line work. These exterior units are usually geometric, but life forms are not uncommon. All of the designs are executed in black paint. The interior of bowls usually has an undecorated field at the bottom, most commonly

Photo 7. Pinedale Black-on-red. *The two examples presented here have a true orange slip, although a red slip is also common, as found on Pinedale Polychrome. Pinedale as a type can best be identified by the individual unit designs on the exterior of the vessels. These often resemble ownership marks of signatures, although they are often repeated around the exterior of the vessel. The small jar in Example 2 exhibits a small butterfly painted on the shoulder and has a finger lug that is a zoomorphic representation, probably a dog's head.*

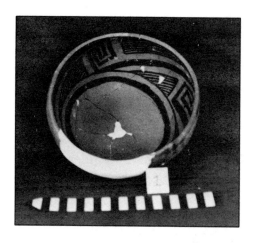

Photo 7a. Interior of bowl in Photo 7. *This exhibits classic Pinedale Style.*

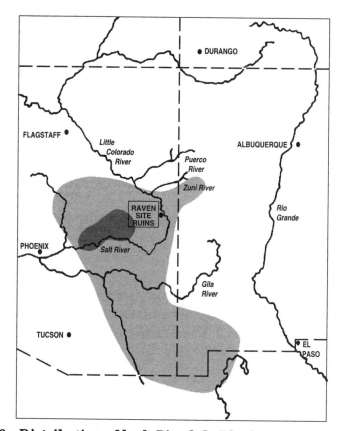

Figure 8. Distribution of both Pinedale Black-on-red and Pinedale Polychrome. *Raven Site Ruins are on the very eastern edge of this distribution area. (From Carlson 70)*

circular. Occasionally the entire interior vessel is decorated. Hachuring and banding lines are of the same width, usually executed with wide, bold units. Pinedale Black-on-red is most frequently decorated in either the Tularosa Style or the Pinedale Style.

DISTRIBUTION — Pinedale Black-on-red shares the same distribution area as Pinedale Polychrome. The core area is to the west and slightly south of Raven Site Ruins.

REMARKS — Pinedale Black-on-red is most easily recognized by the unit designs on the exterior of the vessels. These are often in isolation and very asymmetrical. These units are usually geometric, although life forms are not uncommon.

PINEDALE POLYCHROME

DATES — Pinedale Polychrome was produced between A.D. 1275 and A.D. 1325. These are based upon tree-ring dates from Pinedale Pueblo (Haury/Hargrave 31). Both Pinedale Polychrome and Cedar Creek Polychrome, the next ceramic type in this series, are transitional to Fourmile Polychrome which is the last type in the White Mountain Red Ware sequence. The Pinedale ceramics were produced very briefly in time, only about fifty years, and their presence is very useful when dating the floor of a room or an archaeological level on the site.

CONSTRUCTION — Vessels were made using the coil and scrap method. The body of the clay ranges from grey to buff to reddish brown. A dark center core is sometimes present. The temper is either ground sherds or crushed rock. The slip is usually a good true red or a true orange. The examples in the White Mountain Archaeological Centers Collections are almost all a true red. The slip is usually thick. The black paint ranges from a vitreous shiny black, high in copper and manganese, to a dull organic brown. The white paint is kaolin.

FORM — Bowls are usually medium depth and rounded. Rims of bowls are rounded and sometimes exhibit an external lip. To date, no examples of jars have been found at Raven Site Ruins.

PAINTED DESIGNS — Bowl interiors and exteriors are decorated and jar exteriors. Black-on-red interior designs are common, accompanied by either just white exterior designs, or black outlined in white exterior designs. This thin white border around the black designs will later become a common design element in the next ceramic types in this sequence, specifically significant with the Fourmile Polychromes. The exterior designs on the bowls are very unit in appearance. They resemble ownership marks or makers marks. These emblems are executed in a variety of ways using geometric forms and very often life

Photo 8. Pinedale Polychrome bowl fragments. *White paint is often included on the interior of bowls along with the black designs. The exterior designs are very "unit" in appearance, and they are only rarely connected by line work. Black elemental units outlined in white are common, as are units solely in white kaolin paint. Example 1 uses a white and red interior slip. The squiggles in black on the white slip in Example 1 are classic Pinedale Style. Example 3 exhibits white paint outlining black designs on the interior. Example 3 could be typed as Cedar Creek Polychrome, and not Pinedale Polychrome.*

forms such as snakes, butterflies and birds. Sometimes only white paint is used, sometimes black paint outlined or accented in white.

An important painted design element that now appears with the Pinedale Polychromes can be found on the exterior of many bowls. There is often present a band or line of black paint around the rim of the bowl. This black band is often outlined with white kaolin paint as are many of the other additional design units. Notice how the use of this black banding line develops with the introduction of the next ceramic types in the White Mountain Red Ware sequence, specifically the Fourmile Polychromes. Bowl interiors are most commonly painted in a true Tularosa Style, often with the bottom of the bowls left undecorated.

DISTRIBUTION — Pinedale Polychrome pottery shares the same distribution area as Pinedale Black-on-red (see Figure 8). The core area lies just south and west of Raven Site Ruins. This ceramic type is rarely found very far east of the Little Colorado River.

REMARKS — Pinedale Polychrome vessels are clearly transitional to the remaining White Mountain Red Wares, that is Cedar Creek Polychrome and more importantly, Fourmile Polychrome. Many of the design elements that are specific to the Fourmile Polychromes can be seen in their infancy painted on the Pinedale Polychrome pottery vessels. Specifically, the black band, edged in white, encircling the exterior of bowls near the rim. With the Pinedale Polychromes, we now see all three colors, the red, the black and the white used on all surfaces and in many combinations.

Photo 8a. Exterior of vessels shown in Photo 8. *Unit designs in white, or black and white, paint are diagnostic to the type.*

Photo 8b. Pinedale Polychrome bowl, *interior.*

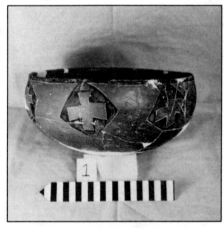

Photo 8c. Pinedale Polychrome bowl *exterior from Photo 8b. The outlined crosses and the upper banding line is often seen on this ceramic type.*

With the next ceramic types in this White Mountain Red Ware sequence that we will examine, the unit elements or ownership marks on the exterior of bowls, will widen and become closer together, creating an exterior design field which will be enclosed at both the top and the bottom by two black bands edged in white.

CEDAR CREEK POLYCHROME

DATES — Cedar Creek Polychrome dates between A.D. 1300 and A.D. 1375. This ceramic type slightly overlaps Pinedale Polychrome earlier, and it precedes the development of the Fourmile Polychromes (Morris 57). Cedar Creek Polychrome may have been discontinued before A.D. 1375, as it is very scarce on sites where the Fourmile Polychromes are discovered. When Cedar Creek Polychrome is discovered on the floor of a room, or at a specific level of excavation, care should be taken not to date the room/level toward the later end of the temporal sequence for this ceramic type. Dates of A.D. 1300 to A.D. 1350 might be a better temporal parameter for this ceramic type.

CONSTRUCTION — Vessels were made using the coil and scrape method. The paste can be many colors including grey, buff, white, or red to brown. The temper is usually ground sherds, although ground rock is sometimes used.

The slip color is usually red (Carlson 70), however, the examples so far discovered at Raven Site Ruins are more commonly red to orange. The predominance of an orange slip has been noted on several of the polychrome ceramics from Raven Site Ruins including Wingate Polychrome, Pinedale Black-on-red, Springerville Polychrome, and now Cedar Creek Polychrome. The White Mountain Red Wares from Raven Site Ruins that exhibit a true red slip are Puerco Black-on-red, St. Johns Black-on-red and St. Johns Polychrome (there is however, tremendous variation in slip color on St. Johns Polychrome from Raven Site Ruins, but usually the color goes from red to brown, not orange), Pinedale Polychrome and the Fourmile Polychromes.

Cedar Creek Polychrome slips are thick and well polished. The white slipped areas that sometimes appear on jar necks and bodies are sometimes granular. This is probably because when the white kaolin is thickly applied, less polishing retains more of the white color, and results in the granular, less polished appearance. Bowls are slipped red/orange on the interior and exterior, jars on the exterior. Jars occasionally will exhibit an area of white slip.

The black paint is black and often vitreous. If this black is applied over an area of white, the edges of the black will often appear greenish. The white paint is kaolin.

FORM — Bowls are medium depth, rounded, with rounded bottoms. Bowls in-curve at the rim. Jars have either vertical necks or no necks at all with out-curved lips.

PAINTED DESIGNS — Bowls are painted on the interior and exterior, jars on the exterior. The dipper shown in Photo 9 is painted on the interior and on the handle. The handle is painted in black with a life form of a centipede. This dipper could be a Pinedale Polychrome (Pinedale Polychromes often exhibit life forms) and not a Cedar Creek Polychrome, or it could be transitional between the two types.

Bowls have either black-on-red/orange interiors and black and white-on-red/orange exteriors, or all three colors on interior and the exterior. Jars have all three colors on the exterior.

The motifs on bowl exteriors are usually broad black units with a narrow white outline. White and black dots are often used to accentuate these designs.

Cedar Creek Polychrome is decorated in Pinedale Style, but the motifs are usually more elaborate than Pinedale Polychrome or Pinedale Black-on-red. During this temporal period the Tularosa Style has completely disappeared from use.

The important design change to notice is the increased use of a black band around the top of the bowl which is edged in white. Another black band often can be seen around the body of the bowl which creates a very linear field of design several inches wide completely encircling the vessel. What has happened is that the isolated units or ownership marks that we observed on Pinedale vessels, have expanded, become more linear. They now touch and completely encircle the vessel exterior. These black bands with their white edge later become an important diagnostic tool in the recognition of the next ceramic type in the White Mountain Red Ware sequence, i.e., the Fourmile Polychromes.

DISTRIBUTION — Cedar Creek Polychrome is found in basically the same areas as the Pinedale and Fourmile Polychromes. The core area of distribution is south and west of Raven Site Ruins. It has not been found east of the Little Colorado River in New Mexico.

REMARKS — Cedar Creek Polychrome is rare at Raven Site Ruins. This is most likely because only a very small area of this 800 room pueblo has been excavated. This sampling bias will undoubtedly disappear as excavations continue. All of the White Mountain Red Wares have been found at the site, but in varying frequencies. For example, St. Johns Polychrome is very abundant, literally tons of sherds have been excavated along with many whole or restorable vessels. This

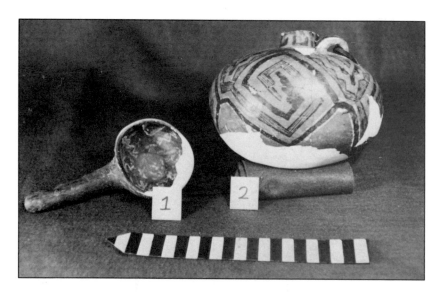

Photo 9. Cedar Creek Polychrome dipper and canteen. *It is very difficult to definitively type the dipper and canteen. They could be anything from St. Johns Polychrome or Pinedale Polychrome, to what we are typing them—Cedar Creek Polychrome. This definition is primarily based upon the use of the white paint to outline the black designs. They are probably transitional from Pinedale Polychrome to Cedar Creek Polychrome. They lack the classic Pinedale Polychrome designs—unit elements and line work.*

Photo 9a. Cedar Creek Polychrome bowl sections, *interior. Example 2 could be a late Pinedale Polychrome.*

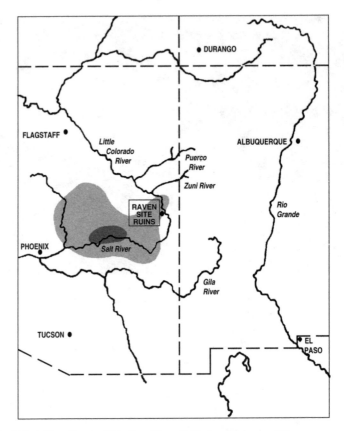

Figure 9. Distribution of Cedar Creek Polychrome. *The core area is south and west of Raven Site Ruins. Raven Site Ruins contain Cedar Creek Polychrome only rarely, although Fourmile Polychrome ceramics are common. (From Carlson 70)*

could indicate a large, ceramic producing population at the site during this temporal period, that is, A.D. 1175 to A.D. 1300. Excavators have recovered very few examples of Pinedale and Cedar Creek ceramics, but interestingly, large amounts of Fourmile Polychrome, the next ceramic type in the sequence, have been un-earthed. These variations in ceramic frequencies will, in time, with continued research and excavation, demonstrate populational increases and declines, migrations and abandonments, and trade networks.

FOURMILE POLYCHROME

DATES — Fourmile Polychrome was produced between A.D. 1325 and A.D. 1400 The most accurate dates for Fourmile are from Canyon Creek Ruin. Good tree-ring dates show that Fourmile Polychromes were produced at this site between A.D. 1326 and A.D. 1348 and show that the type was well developed by as early as A.D. 1326 (Haury 34).

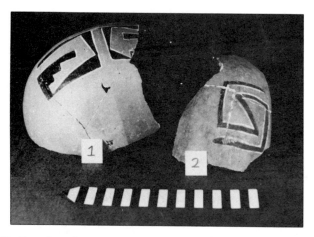

Photo 9b. Cedar Creek Polychrome exterior of large bowl fragments *shown in Photo 9a. Example 1 demonstrates how the unit elements that we have observed on Pinedale Polychrome vessels are now becoming wider, less isolated and enveloping more of the exterior of the vessel.*

The Fourmile Polychromes overlap Cedar Creek Polychromes temporally, and if large amounts of either type are found in any quantity on a site, the other type is rare at the same site. This seems also to be true at Raven Site Ruins, where large amounts of Fourmile Polychrome are present, and Cedar Creek is virtually absent.

CONSTRUCTION — Vessels were made using the coil and scrape method. The body of the clay is white, buff or grey. The temper is almost always crushed sherds and inclusions are small white/red (sometimes black) fragments.

The slip color is usually a good red, although an orange is not uncommon. The slip is thick, well polished, and is made from yellow limonite (Haury and Hargrave 31). Bowls are slipped on the interior and exterior and jars on the exterior. Jars usually have a white slipped area on the upper shoulders and neck. This use of the white slip on the upper areas of jars will tend to cause some confusion when we examine the next pottery type in the series, i.e., Showlow Polychrome.

The black paint is a glaze, or matte glaze which is often vitreous. This black will often appear greenish, especially when it is applied over white. This black paint is composed of lead, copper and manganese (Haury and Hargrave 31). The white paint is chalky, almost fugitive in that it barely survives preservation. The white paint is kaolin. Carlson reports that some of the Fourmile vessels that he examined exhibited a purple paint in addition to the black and white (Carlson 70). No examples of this purple color have been discovered, to date, at Raven Site Ruins.

The vessel is slipped first with the red background color, and white in the case of the shoulders and necks of jars. Then the white paint is applied first as an outline to the black designs. The black paint was then applied, leaving just a fine line of white showing as a border. One of the bowls shown in Photo 10d exhibits a very interesting paint application. The white on the exterior of the bowl was applied over some type of masking, which was later removed, leaving a crisp red unpainted area.

FORM — Bowls are usually medium depth with in-curved rims. They have rounded sides and bottoms. Bowls often have internal bevels and are thickened near the rim. The rim is often flattened, this allows the artist to add the often present ticking designs found on the rim of bowls. Small "flower pot" bowls and square bowls have also been reported (Martin and Willis 40), although with the exception of one sherd segment, no examples of these forms have yet been discovered at Raven Site Ruins. Jars are usually very short and globular with short necks or virtually no necks at all, the body of the jar goes immediately to a flared lip.

PAINTED DESIGNS — Bowls are painted on the exterior and interior and jars on the exterior. Example 3 in Photo 10c shows a bowl with no interior paint except for the black banding line at the top interior. This is very much the exception in the examples from Raven Site Ruins. However, Carlson reports several vessels from the collections that he examined with no interior paint except this band (Carlson 70). Bowls usually have both black and white paint on the interior and exterior, but it is not uncommon to find interiors of bowls with only the black painted designs. Usually a thin white line borders the black designs on the interior and exterior of bowls. This is particularly true of the banding lines, and is diagnostic to the type. If you find a sherd with a black band around the rim and this black band has a thin white accompanying band usually on the bottom side of the black from the rim, and it is a red vessel, then you can almost always accurately type the sherd as a Fourmile Polychrome. This is also often true if the sherd is not a rim piece. Fourmile Polychromes usually have these black designs, that are wide, bold, and edged by a thin line of white kaolin.

The exterior of bowls usually have a design field completely encircling the bowl, that is bordered on the top and bottom by a black banding line edged in white. Within this bordered design field white paint is used in a variety of ways, often including interlocked "F" hooks, plain parallel lines and spiraling triangles. It is not uncommon to find black painted designs incorporated with the fine white lines within this exterior design field.

***Photo 10 (interiors and exteriors above). Fourmile Polychrome bowls
and large glue-up fragments.*** *The most important painted design combination to recognize in the identification of Fourmile Polychrome are the wide
black units that are edged with a thin white line, particularly on the rim bands,
interior and exterior. These beautiful vessels were produced near the pinnacle
of ceramic technology for the White Mountain Red Ware series. During this
time, the artists began to paint depictions of legends, and illustrate stories on
the surface of these ceramics. The Fourmile Polychromes lack the symmetry of
the earlier ceramics we have examined. This lack of symmetry has caused
researchers to begin to recognize the symbols represented are meaningful
rather than just fanciful.*

Bowl interiors combine both black and white paint (and sometimes
other new vitreous colors, such as purple and green) in a tremendous
variety of ways. The most important design change with the Fourmile
Polychromes, is the almost total lack of symmetry on bowl interiors.
Even bowl exteriors often lack symmetry in spite of their controlled
design field. The interior designs of bowls will fill the bottom with
birds, terraced units, crosses and curls. The black paint used to create

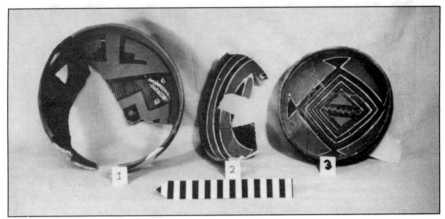

Photo 10a. Fourmile Polychrome bowls. *The interior of Examples 1 and 3 exhibit meaningful symbols (see Symbols, page 139).*

Photo 10b. Exterior of Fourmile Polychrome bowls in Photo 10a. *Fourmile Polychrome vessel exteriors will often exhibit symmetry around the entire vessel with the exception of one small unit area.*

these images is often edged in white, but not always. Sometimes solo white units of design appear on bowl interiors.

The Fourmile Polychrome vessels are among the finest ever produced in the White Mountain Red Ware series. Radical changes occurred in the design elements, exemplified by the lack of symmetry. This lack of symmetry is largely because the artists were doing more than just decorating a vessel. In many cases, for the first time, the potters were depicting stories and legends on the ceramics. The characters depicted and the elements of the narrative are depicted using a simple logographic language. These early depictions are believed to be associated with the development of the Katsina Cult in the White Mountains of Arizona (Adams 91). These symbols and their meanings are discussed in *Symbols,* page 139.

Photo 10c. Interior of Fourmile Polychrome bowls and large glue-up section. *Example 1 shows the asymmetry common to Fourmile Polychromes and Example 3 is left completely unpainted on the interior. This unpainted example is unusual.*

Photo 10d. Exterior of Fourmile Polychrome bowls *in Photo 10c. Example 1 demonstrates the common interlocked "F" motif. Vessel 3 was executed in a very unusual way. The zig-zag around the bowl was masked off, then the white kaolin paint was applied. The masking was then removed.*

DISTRIBUTION — Fourmile Polychromes are principally found south and west of Raven Site Ruins. They actually have a wider distribution than was previously understood. Whole vessels have been discovered at Homolovi Ruin near Winslow, Arizona. This expands the distribution area to the north of the core area. The discovery of abundant Fourmile material at Raven Site Ruins expands the distribution area even further east.

REMARKS — Large amounts of Fourmile Polychrome have been discovered in the north pueblo at Raven Site Ruins. Fine examples have also been excavated from the south pueblo, although they were

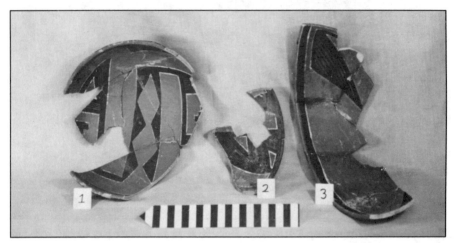

Photo 10e. Fourmile Polychrome bowl sections. *This ceramic type is found in the north pueblo at Raven Site Ruins. Vessels are usually widely scattered over large areas, as if they were deliberately smashed in a ritual "kill".*

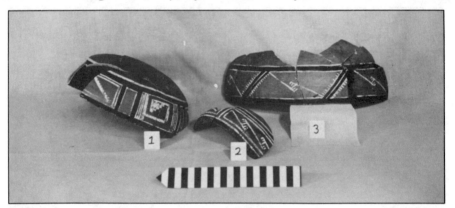

Photo 10f. Exterior of Fourmile Polychrome bowls *in Photo 10e.*

not produced there. The inhabitants of the south pueblo post-date the production of the Fourmile Polychromes. They retained the vessels as heirloom pieces, and even tried to copy the form and colors, although rather unsuccessfully.

Most of the Fourmile Polychrome material recovered from Raven Site Ruins is spread over a very wide area of the north pueblo. A sherd or two of a vessel will be discovered, then years later, with the excavation of a room or area of the pueblo many meters away, other sherds from the same vessel will be discovered. These bowls seem to have been deliberately smashed in a ritual "killing" of the bowl. Other forms of vessel "killing" include punching a hole in the bottom, rim notching and rim mutilation. This "killing" of the vessel releases the spirit of the vessel. Later, the development of the "spirit break", a painted band

Photo 10g. Interior of Fourmile Polychrome bowl and large bowl sections.

Photo 10h. Fourmile Polychrome bowl and large glue-up sections. Exteriors of examples in 10g.

which includes a gap, executed around the body of the vessel was created which replaced the need to break the piece. The Fourmile Polychromes from Raven Site Ruins may have been used in a ceremony similar to one that was observed by Cushing at Zuni Pueblo in the 19th century. The women would leave their very finest pottery outside the rooftop entrances on a certain ceremonial evening. The Katsina clowns would come around rooftop to rooftop and smash the vessels (Cushing 79).

Fourmile Polychromes are an exciting find during excavation. These beautiful ceramics depict stories and legends and the very beginnings of a written language in the prehistoric Southwest. They are also integrated into the origins of the Katsina Cult which developed in the White Mountain area, along the Little Colorado River during this temporal period. Each year at Raven Site Ruins, as the excavations proceed, as the layers left by time are peeled away by the archaeologists' trowels, we anxiously await the appearance of a Fourmile Polychrome bowl with it's prehistoric story to tell the modern world.

SHOWLOW POLYCHROME

DATES — The dates for Showlow Polychromes are the same as for Fourmile Polychromes, i.e., A.D. 1325 to A.D. 1400 (Carlson 70). What we are going to discover, as we examine this ceramic type, is that the Showlow Polychromes and Fourmile Polychromes are virtually identical except that there is more use of a white slip on the Showlow Polychromes, especially in the case of bowl interiors which are often slipped white on the entire surface. Showlow Polychrome is undoubtedly a late temporal development from the Fourmile Polychrome ceramics. It must date at least at the upper end of the temporal realm of the Fourmiles. The Point of Pines Phase at Point of Pines, dates this

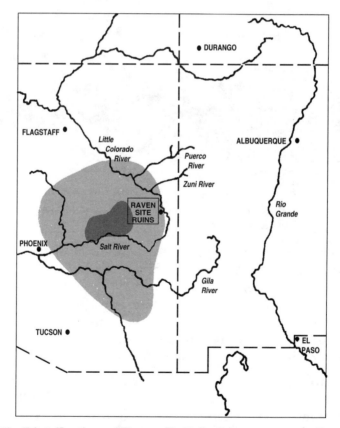

Figure 10. Distribution of Fourmile Polychrome pottery. *Recent excavations have expanded this distribution area north and east. (From Carlson 70)*

ceramic type between A.D. 1400 A.D. and A.D. 1450. This matches what we seem to be observing at Raven Site Ruins. We don't have any Showlow Polychrome vessels. We have not discovered any ceramics that look like Fourmile Polychromes, except that they have increased use of white slip, i. e., Showlow Polychromes. This is probably because, as we have discussed previously, that the White Mountain Red Ware ceramic tradition ended at Raven Site Ruins during the Fourmile ceramic production phase. Sometime between A.D. 1325 and A.D. 1350+. This could preclude any development/production of a Showlow Polychrome at Raven Site Ruins, because no late Fourmile Polychromes were produced at the site.

Remember that ceramic production continued at Raven Site Ruins long after A.D. 1350, with the introduction of Heshotauthla Polychromes and then a whole new series of ceramics, i.e., the Zuni Glaze Wares (see *Zuni Glaze Wares,* page 58). It is entirely possible that the Raven Site Ruins, north pueblo potters, who were making the Fourmile Polychromes, moved north to Homolovi around A.D. 1350, as is substantiated by the abandonment phase of the north pueblo. These potters continued to produce ceramics in the White Mountain Red Ware tradition, including the Showlow Polychromes, using local clays and tempers. These late Fourmile to Showlow Polychrome ceramics at Homolovi temporally overlap with the Sikyatki ceramic assemblages, i.e., the early Hopi Yellow Wares. Both the Sikyatki material and Fourmile ceramics are believed to be associated with the development and expansion of the Katsina Cult.

CONSTRUCTION — Vessels were created using the coil and scrape method. The body of the clay is the same as found in the Fourmile ceramics, buff to grey and white. Temper is ground sherd. Bowls exhibit either an overall white slip or a part red and white slip, interior. The exterior of bowls has an overall red slip. Jars have a white slip that is predominant, with a red slip that extends from the base of the jar to the middle body. A white slip is used on the upper body of jars and on the neck and shoulders. The black paint is glaze, it can appear green or even purple, depending upon the firing. The white paint is kaolin and is applied after the red slip. The white is used to designate the black motifs, the black paint is then applied.

FORM — Bowls are medium depth with rounded sides and bases and rounded bottoms. They in-curve at the rim. Jars have a globular body and short neck.

PAINTED DESIGNS — Bowl interiors and exteriors are painted, as are jar exteriors. Bowl interiors show an increase in white paint. The white slip/paint is applied over the red slip to create the design field for the later applied black paint. Some bowls are not entirely slipped white on the interior, but will leave an area of the red slip showing. Bowl exteriors are virtually identical to Fourmile Polychromes. Wide black banding lines create a design field around the body of the bowl, one at the rim and one several centimeters lower. These black banding lines are edged by a thin white line, and the designs within this field are often created with these thin white lines of kaolin paint. Black paint often appears with the white, within these banding lines on the exterior of bowls. The interlocked "F" motif is common.

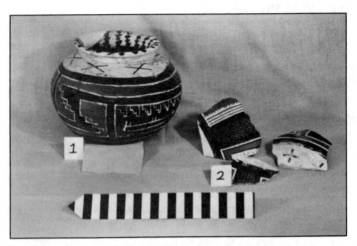

Photo 11. Showlow Polychrome/Late Fourmile Polychrome Jar. *The increased use of white paint on the upper regions of jars and on the interior of bowls designates these vessels as Showlow Polychrome as opposed to Fourmile Polychromes.*

Bowl interiors exhibit the same lack of symmetry that we have observed with the Fourmile Polychromes, and similar motifs. Because so few vessels have been examined, it is difficult to determine whether or not there is a true shift of style from the Fourmile Polychrome Style to something new. The design motifs on the interior of Showlow Polychrome very much resemble those exhibited on Point of Pines Polychrome, the next ceramic type that we will discuss. There is an overall reduction of artistry. The designs are reduced. They are simple and often even crude.

DISTRIBUTION — Showlow Polychrome can be found in the same areas as Fourmile Polychrome. Few examples of this ceramic type occur at any one site. Showlow Polychromes are found at Homolovi which extends the distribution northward. This type is most frequently found below the Mogollon rim.

REMARKS — What is important to observe about Showlow Polychrome and the types differentiation from Fourmile Polychrome, is the increased use of a white slip on large areas of the vessels. The use of a white slip to cover the entire interior of bowls is an interesting development which occurs on many ceramic types about the same time in prehistory. Kwakina Polychrome, one of the Zuni Glaze Wares which we will examine, exhibits this same color shift, from a bowl that is slipped entirely in red and then painted with designs, to one that is slipped red on the outside and white on the interior before designs are added. Kwakina Polychrome was produced at the same time as the Showlow Polychromes. Kwakina Polychrome is abundant at Raven Site Ruins, as are Fourmile Polychromes; all of these types overlap temporally. Another ceramic type produced south of Raven Site Ruins, and often traded to Raven Site were the Gila Polychromes. These exhibit the same white interior treatment, and also appear during the same time period.

The increase in the use of the white slip on the interior of bowls after

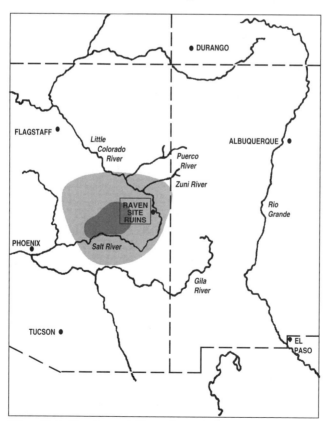

Figure 11. The distribution of Showlow Polychrome. *The core area lies south and west of Raven Site Ruins. (From Carlson 70)*

A.D. 1325 by various groups over a wide area, could be related to the development of the vitreous, glaze paints. By increasing the amounts of copper and manganese in the pigments, the potters discovered that, when fired, these become bright glassy colors that vary from strong black to greens and even purple.

These strong colors are more attractive on a white surface, rather than the previous traditional red, and more color variation is achieved in firing when these new glaze paints are applied to a white slip. As we examine even later ceramic types, we will observe an increase in the use of white slips and glaze paints, even to the point where the entire bowl is slipped white, and the red bowl slips are discontinued. (see Zuni Glaze Wares, page 58).

POINT OF PINES POLYCHROME

DATES — Point of Pines Polychrome dates between A.D. 1400 and A.D. 1450. These dates are not based on good tree-ring samples, but rather on the disappearance of Fourmile Polychrome by the year A.D. 1400 when the Point of Pines Polychromes appear. The absence of intrusive Hopi and Zuni Glaze Wares (post-A.D. 1450 wares) at the Point of Pines sites gives us the terminal date (Morris 57).

Point of Pines is a prehistoric copy of a Fourmile Polychrome, made by a group of people who probably had never made painted ceramics before. Therefore, on sites where both types are found, the makers of the Fourmile Polychromes would have had to have already abandoned the site sometime before A.D. 1400, and the makers of the Point of Pines Polychromes would have arrived and re-occupied the same site. They attempted to copy the fine work of the Fourmile potters, with limited success.

At Raven Site Ruins, both ceramic types are found. The north pueblo at the site contains the fine Fourmile Polychromes and the south pueblo at the same location is where the Point of Pines Polychromes have been excavated. The north pueblo was all but abandoned between A.D. 1350 and A.D. 1400, and the south pueblo was built sometime after A.D. 1350.

The south pueblo inhabitants produced a series of ceramics called the Zuni Glaze Wares. These use primarily a white slip rather than a red slip. After A.D. 1330 the use of the red slips declined and were eventually discontinued.

CONSTRUCTION — Vessels were created using the coil and scrape method. The body of the clay is usually brown and sometimes grey. The inclusions in the clay are very sharp and angular. These appear to be sand or scoria. Ground sherds are not used.

Bowls are slipped red on the interior and exterior, although these attempts to produce a red slip often fail. The result is a brown or brown to orange vessel. Jars are slipped red on the body. The shoulders and neck are slipped white.

The polish on these vessels is rough, even lumpy. It is uneven and poorly executed, especially on the lower portions of the ceramics. Large fire clouds will often obliterate the painted designs.

The black paint quality varies from a good matte glaze to a watery brown. It often appears thin and poorly mixed. The kaolin white paint is very fugitive and thin. As with the Fourmile Polychromes, the white

12a

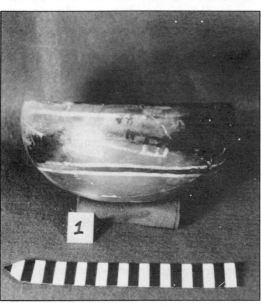

12b

Photo 12a interior & 12b exterior. Point of Pines Polychrome bowl with bird motif. *This ceramic type is a prehistoric copy of a Fourmile Polychrome. Both Fourmile and Point of Pines ceramics are found at Raven Site Ruins. The potters who produced the Fourmile ceramics could not have been present on the site at the same time as the potters that produced the Point of Pines Polychromes. If they had been, they would have been greatly amused by these poor attempts at reproducing their technology.*

paint is applied before the black, the black is then applied leaving a border of white remaining to outline the motifs.

FORM — Bowls are globular and medium depth. They in-curve at the rim. Rims are sometimes flattened, and slight beveling on the inside of the rim is not uncommon.

No examples of jars have been discovered, to date, at Raven Site Ruins. Carlson reports that jars are large with high rounded shoulders and short necks that taper inward toward the rim (Carlson 70).

PAINTED DESIGNS — Bowl interiors and exteriors are painted, as well as jar exteriors. The designs mimic the Fourmile Polychromes. The exterior of bowls use the same banding lines edged with white, creating a design field around the body of bowl several centimeters wide. Inside this design field thin white lines are used to create designs, including the frequent use of the interlocked "F" pattern. Black paint is sometimes included in this design work.

The interior of bowls again copies the Fourmile artistry. Bird motifs and other life forms occur as well as geometric patterns. These are usually executed very poorly. The paint is sloppy, quickly applied, and the artist often leaves large areas of the vessel unpainted while at the same time cramming designs into a single area. The design style can best be described as degenerative Fourmile.

DISTRIBUTION — Point of Pines Polychrome has been found around the Point of Pines area of Arizona, and just south of Point of Pines near Nantack Ridge (Wasley 52). The discovery of this type at Raven Site Ruins along the Little Colorado River between St. Johns and Springerville, Arizona, expands this distribution to the north and east.

REMARKS — Point of Pines Polychrome is best described as a degenerative Fourmile, not only in style, but also in paste, slip, temper and all of the techniques necessary to produce a fine pottery.

There is an overall decline in ceramic technology by the year A.D. 1400 in the White Mountain area. The glaze paints could be considered a technological advancement because of the bright colors that they produce. The shift from a red slipped vessel to a white slip overall is probably due to the increased beauty of these glaze paints on the white slip. However, there is a technical problem with the glaze paints. During firing, the paint runs and blurs. The artist who spent hours and hours painting a detailed design on her pottery would be disappointed after the vessel came out of the firing. The colors are bright and glassy, but her designs would have run together and become obliterated.

The shift to the use of the glaze paints is probably responsible for the decrease in the fine artistry that we have observed before the year A.D. 1400. The lack of fine artistry observed on the Point of Pines Polychrome may be a reflection of this decrease in the fine line work as a ceramic technique after A.D. 1400.

South Pueblo, Raven Site Ruins showing the large diversity of ceramic types discovered at the site.

Chapter 5

The Zuni Glaze Wares
of Raven Site Ruins

The Zuni Glaze Wares begin with an increased use of vitreous and glassy pigments around the year A.D. 1325. These pigments are sometimes found on a few of the later White Mountain Red Wares, but they are never the principle pigment that was employed, and they are usually used to enhance the vessel designs with dots or other limited applications. These glaze paints run when they are fired, often obliterating the artist's fine brush work. However, these glaze paints produce brilliant colors of greens and even purples when applied to a white slip. Often the white slip constituents meld with the paint producing unplanned color variations. As we proceed through the Zuni Glaze Wares, notice the increased use of the white slip, first on the interior of the vessels (in the case of bowls) and later on both the interior and exterior.

HESHOTAUTHLA POLYCHROME

DATES — This very important polychrome was produced at Raven Site Ruins between A.D. 1300 and A.D. 1400. (Woodbury/Woodbury 66). Carlson reports that the type dates only between A.D. 1300 and

Photo 13. Heshotauthla Polychromes, interiors. The classic Heshotauthla bowls in design and form can be seen, with glaze paint interiors. Heshotauthla and Pinedale Polychromes are close cousins temporally and stylistically.

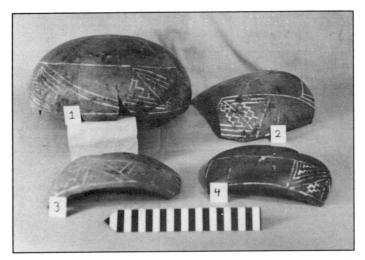

Photo 13a. Heshotauthla Polychromes, exteriors *of those vessel fragments shown in Photo 13. The white kaolin paint is applied thin and the lines are very fine, often with isolated geometric units linked around the body of the bowl.*

A.D. 1375 (Carlson 70). Heshotauthla Polychrome certainly appears around A.D. 1300 as we will see by the transition from the St. Johns/ Springerville Polychromes to this type based on the exterior use of color and design. Heshotauthla also uses a design layout on the interior of bowls that very much resembles the Pinedale Style, although less complex. Carlson reports that Heshotauthla also sometimes exhibits a Tularosa Style on the interior of bowls (Carlson 70).

The reason why Heshotauthla Polychrome is an important ceramic type in the White Mountains, and at Raven Site Ruins, is because it overlaps temporally with several of the White Mountain Red Wares, including St. Johns Polychrome, Springerville Polychrome, Pinedale Polychrome, Cedar Creek, and even Fourmile. All of these White Mountain Red Wares show a developmental sequence of style and design changes, basically one to the other over time. Many in the series do overlap temporally, and they were produced contemporaneously, but still, there is a continuity that can be observed.

Heshotauthla Polychrome has one distinguishing characteristic that can easily be recognized, black glaze paint on the interior of bowls and the exterior of jars. This is a true, glassy black. It is thick, shiny, and the line work is sloppy, poorly executed, and this paint runs together when fired. This black paint often will appear greenish, or even purple.

The invention of this black paint, high in copper, around the year A.D. 1300, caused a split in the ceramic traditions that were being followed at Raven Site Ruins. One group of potters continued to produce the

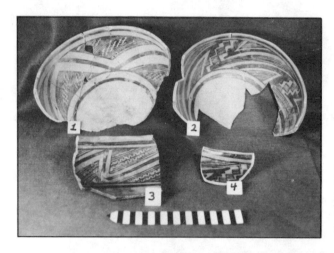

Photo 13b. Hesho-tauthla Polychrome bowl sections, interiors with glaze paint and open bottoms.

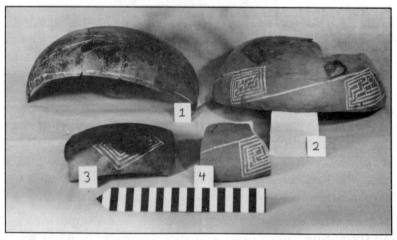

Photo 13c. Exterior of the bowl sections of Heshotauthla Polychrome bowl sections, exteriors of those shown in Photo 13b. Notice the very fine white line work. The kaolin paint did not run when fired and these are the only fine brush strokes that were possible.

White Mountain Red Wares. This series of ceramics concluded at Raven Site Ruins with the Fourmile and Showlow Polychromes around the year A.D. 1400. For around one hundred years, the White Mountain Red Ware potters knew about this new paint and they occasionally used it to create a shiny or glassy effect on small areas of a design, often with the use of dots and occasionally to enhance the color of a banding line, as is often seen on the later Fourmile Polychromes. But they never accepted this new paint as a primary vehicle to create their designs. They never used this new copper concentrated pigment for the majority of their work because it runs when it is fired. You can imagine the frustration of the prehistoric potter who would spend countless hours carefully painting an intricate design on a Fourmile

Polychrome using the new glaze paint, only to have her creation ruined in the firing process and all of her work run together in a blurry mess of glassy color.

Another group of potters admired these new pigments enough to ignore tradition, and begin an entirely new ceramic series, i.e., the Zuni Glaze Wares. This Zuni Glaze Ware series technically begins with Heshotauthla Polychrome around the year A.D. 1300.

Both the White Mountain Red Ware ceramics and the Zuni Glaze Wares were produced side by side at Raven Site Ruins for nearly one hundred years. Around A.D. 1400 the White Mountain Red Ware potters moved from the site, probably to Homolovi near the present day Winslow, Arizona. The Zuni Glaze Ware potters continued to inhabit Raven Site Ruins, and produce their pottery, until possibly as late as A.D. 1475.

CONSTRUCTION — Vessels are created using the coil and scrape method. The body of the clay is light grey or buff. Many vessels from Raven Site Ruins have black paste. The temper is usually finely ground sherds, inclusions are angular.

Bowls are slipped red on the interior and exterior, jars on the exterior. This red slip often appears orange or reddish brown. The polishing on bowls and jars is well-executed and smooth.

Photo 13d. Heshotauthla Polychrome jar and jar sections. *The excavations from Raven Site Ruins have produced very few jars other than Tularosa Black-on-white (see Cibola White Wares). This example of a Heshotauthla Polychrome jar is one of the few in the White Mountain Archaeological Center's Collections.*

The black paint is thick, glassy and high in copper content. It often appears bubbly. It will often appear greenish or even purple. The white paint is kaolin and is usually thin, streaky and chalky, although it is less fugitive than is found on St. Johns Polychrome.

FORM — Bowls are usually medium depth with rounded sides. These curve in at the rim. Rims are usually rounded, although an occasional specimen will exhibit flattening. The bowls are thickest near the rim. Bottoms are rounded. Jars are rare. One example from Raven Site Ruins has been discovered in the south pueblo. It has a wide mouth and flattened shoulders with a globular base. This jar form seems to be a late development, probably appearing around the year A.D. 1400 or later.

Bowls are painted on the interior and exterior and jars on the exterior. Bowl exteriors are executed principally in white paint although occasionally black painted designs are included with the white. If black paint is included on the exterior, it is usually used to form panel dividers, as in Springerville Polychrome, or to create units which are then outlined in white as in Pinedale Polychrome.

PAINTED DESIGNS — The white designs are created with thin lines in units that are often connected by additional white line work. These white lines are thinner than are found on St. Johns Polychrome and are usually only about 3 millimeters wide. These design units often slightly resemble the unit elements found on Pinedale Polychrome vessels, except that they are almost always simple geometrics, and not life forms. These white designs are almost always concentrated in a narrow band near the rim of the vessel, they rarely invade the body of the bowl as do St. Johns Polychrome exterior designs.

It is interesting to notice the continuation from the early Wingate Polychrome bowls with very wide exterior white designs created using slips, to the narrower white designs found on St. Johns Polychrome, and now the very thin intricate white line work on the Heshotauthla bowl exteriors. It seems that with the use of the uncontrollable glaze paint on the interior of the bowl, the Heshotauthla potters went to intricate extremes with the white paint, which did not run, on the exterior. White paint does not appear on bowl interiors.

Bowl interiors are painted with a thick vitreous black. The paint is often quickly applied. Because this paint runs during firing, the edges of the designs are often spread out and blurred. The design styles used on bowl interiors are sometimes Tularosa but more commonly resemble the Pinedale Style.

There is often a continuous band about half a centimeter below the rim.

This wide band is usually accompanied by a narrower band above and below. The bottom of the bowls are usually left undecorated. Brush work is usually quick and sloppy, but the overall layout is well conceived and symmetrical.

DISTRIBUTION — Heshotauthla has been found at Point of Pines and Bidahochi to the west and as far east as Pecos. The Woodburys also found this type from El Moro to Zuni (Woodbury/Woodbury 66). The abundance of this type at Raven Site Ruins increases the distribution range to the south.

REMARKS — Heshotauthla Polychrome begins a new ceramic tradition. This ceramic type is the first of the Zuni Glaze Wares. The development of the vitreous paints, high in copper content, resulted in a shift from traditional designs and styles to a new series of ceramics in the White Mountains of Arizona. Because the paint runs and blurs when it is fired, the potters could no longer create the intricate line work on the interior of bowls as in the past. This vitreous paint produced brilliant colors that are first seen used in the traditional way on a red slipped vessel, usually resulting in just a shiny black. As the use of these paints continued, potters began to discover how beautiful they became when applied to white slips rather than the standard red. As this ceramic sequence continues we will observe the changes that the prehistoric potters made with slips to accommodate the use of this "new" paint, after A.D. 1300.

HESHOTAUTHLA BLACK-ON-RED

DATES — Heshotauthla Black-on-red shares the same temporal span as Heshotauthla Polychrome, A.D. 1300 to A.D. 1400.

REMARKS — Construction, form, painted designs and distribution of Heshotauthla Black-on-red ceramic vessels is identical in every way to Heshotauthla Polychrome, except that there is no exterior white paint.

To date, no Heshotauthla Black-on-red vessels have been definitively discovered at Raven Site Ruins. Sherds have been found that are Heshotauthla, that are too small to determine if there is the presence of any white external paint, which makes it impossible to determine whether or not they are a polychrome or black-on-red Heshotauthla.

Because of the abundance of Heshotauthla Polychrome at the site, many of these smaller sherds are undoubtedly Heshotauthla Black-on-red.

KWAKINA POLYCHROME

DATES — The estimated dates for Kwakina Polychrome are between A.D. 1325 and A.D. 1400. This type overlaps temporally with a long list of ceramic types from the White Mountains that we have already discussed including both White Mountain Red Wares and now several Zuni Glaze Wares. This clustering of dates beginning around A.D. 1300 and all of them terminating at A.D. 1400, may be slightly artificial. The appearance dates given to this list of ceramic types are most likely correct, i.e., approximately the A.D. 1300 mark, however, terminating the production of many of these ceramic types at A.D. 1400 may be due to a prejudice that has long been present in the academic literature. For many years it was proposed that the prehistoric ruins in the Southwest had all been abandoned by A.D. 1400. How this ceiling of A.D. 1400 first appeared is unclear. Few good tree-ring dates that postdate A.D. 1400 have been excavated. The lack of tree-ring dates after A.D. 1400 is pretty good reason not to date a prehistoric site in the Southwest later than that time. However, let us assume that a prehistoric pueblo was occupied after A.D. 1400. Trees were cut and used in new construction of room blocks, let's say for argument, in the years between A.D. 1470 and A.D. 1520. These new rooms were occupied for a few decades and then after A.D. 1540 the Spanish and Athapaskans invaded the area. Many pueblos were quickly aban-

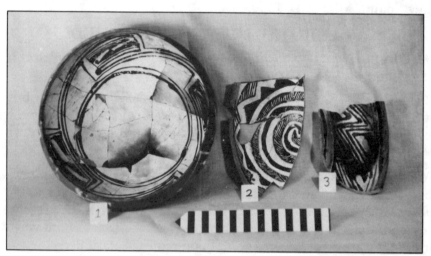

Photo 14. Kwakina Polychrome bowl and large sherds showing interior. *The use of an overall white slip on the interior of bowls differentiates this type from Heshotauthla Polychrome. This overall white slip is probably due to the desire to bring out the glassy glaze colors of the "new" paint discovered around A.D. 1300. Example 3 has the addition of a fugitive red paint on the interior along with the standard glaze color (see Kwakina Polychrome-plus).*

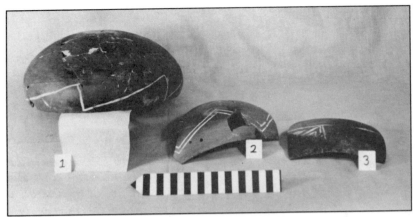

Photo 14a. Kwakina Polychrome bowl, exterior of examples shown in Photo 14. The white kaolin paint is used in an identical way to Heshotauthla Polychrome.

doned. There is not a lot of evidence in the literature from the Spanish conquistadors to support any destruction of pueblos by burning or other methods that would leave archaeological evidence (and carbonized tree-ring dates) that would indicate the true date of these later pueblo occupations.

There is good evidence from the Spanish chronicles of re-use of pueblo materials in the forced construction of missions and other structures that the Spanish felt were necessary for their purposes. Any abandoned pueblo room blocks, that still retained good beam material, would have been scavenged for this precious resource. Good, straight timber must be manuported from the high mountains. This is a labor-intensive process.

The south pueblo at Raven Site Ruins, from the ceramic assemblages, suggests dates that post-date the A.D. 1400 ceiling. Little or no wood has been found in a 400-room block construction area. There had to have been wood beams to support the roofs. We never find any. Not even enough charcoal to suggest it was left in place and burned. Remember that the preservation at Raven Site Ruins is remarkable, an archaeologist's dream. The soil is ph neutral and the hill is well-drained. I suggest that possibly any wood that remained in the abandoned pueblos between A.D. 1400 and A.D. 1540, was re-used by the later inhabitants of the area, i.e., the Spanish Conquistadors, the Spanish settlers that followed them, then the Mormons, etc. This theory is further supported by the fact that a sheepherders dwelling that dates around the 1730s was built not fifty meters from the site, using not only the wooded beams from Raven Site Ruins, but the travertine stone as well.

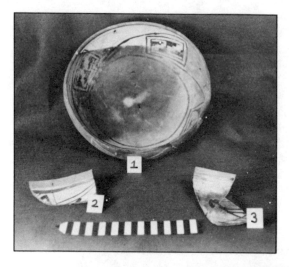

Photo 14b. Kwakina Polychrome bowl and sherds. *The use of the overall white slip on the interior of these bowls accented the vitreous glaze paint.*

Photo 14c. Kwakina Polychrome bowl and shreds, *exteriors of the bowl and sherds shown in Photo 14b.*

CONSTRUCTION — Vessels were produced using the coil and scrape method. The body of the clay is light to dark grey, often with this variation within a single vessel. It can also be tan, pinkish-buff to light brown. Carbon streak is sometimes present. Temper is angular and medium to fine in texture.

The slip is the key to this ceramic type, and why this type is differentiated from Heshotauthla Polychrome. Bowls usually have a complete, or occasionally a partial white slip on the interior. Bowls still have a red slip on the exterior, as is found on Heshotauthla Polychrome. Occasionally there is a band of red on the interior rim of bowls, that has not been slipped white. Jar exteriors are slipped principally red with a zone of white on the body or more commonly around the neck.

The surface of this type is well polished on the red slips, but the white slip is fragile, often not surviving preservation as well as the red. Flaking is common, as is foliation in the white slip areas of the pottery. It seems that with the red slipped areas the prehistoric potters have their systems well developed, but with the new application of large areas of white slip, there are still a few technological problems to solve, such as chalking and flaking.

The black paint is glaze, it ranges from a very dense black to bright green. It often appears bubbly. Woodbury and Woodbury report: *"single brush strokes sometimes begin dull and streaky and end with a blob of heavy glaze."* (Woodbury/Woodbury 66).

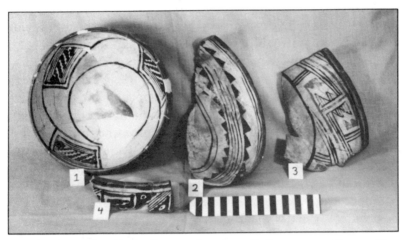

Photo 14d. Kwakina Polychrome bowl and glue-up sections. *Example 3 also has the additional red fugitive paint discussed in "Kwakina Polychrome-plus".*

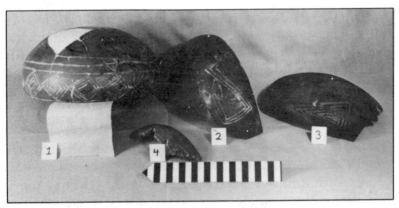

Photo 14e. Kwakina Polychrome bowl and glue-up sections, *exteriors of those shown in Photo 14d. Very similar to Heshotauthla, the white exterior paint is used to create units in narrow white lines that are often linked by lines of the same width.*

The white exterior paint is kaolin. It is chalky and usually frail.

FORM — Bowls are common. The sides of the bowls seem to have an increase in roundness, creating a very globular effect, probably due to an increase in the in-curvature at the rim. The rims of bowls are usually beveled inward. No examples of jars have yet been discovered at Raven Site Ruins. There seems to be an overall absence of jars for many of the ceramic types between A.D. 1300 and A.D. 1400. Jars have been reported to be globular-bodied and straight-necked.

PAINTED DESIGNS — The painted designs on Kwakina Polychrome are nearly identical to Heshotauthla Polychrome, except that bowl interiors are slipped usually with an overall white instead of the earlier red. Bowls still have the red slip on the exterior and these exteriors are decorated with narrow white line motifs very similar to Heshotauthla. The white exterior lines are often grouped into geometric units that are usually connected by additional white line work. Carlson reports that the exterior of bowls usually have black motifs that are outlined in white (Carlson 70), however, no examples demonstrating this use of black have been discovered at Raven Site Ruins and many examples of Kwakina Polychrome have been excavated. Rinaldo reports that he discovered sherds of Kwakina Polychrome with red lines painted on the exterior of bowls that contrast the red slip (Rinaldo 61). The use of a red paint on the exterior of bowls has not been observed at Raven Site Ruins, however, the use of a fugitive red in addition to the black paint on the interior of bowls has frequently been observed.

Bowl interiors usually leave the center of the bowl undecorated. The interior paint is black glaze, often in a very sloppy Pinedale Style. Tularosa Style is sometimes used but not frequently. The use of the black paint on bowl interiors is very quickly executed. The use of space is well-planned, and bowl interiors are usually nicely symmetrical, but the brush work very sloppy. This is largely due to the use of the vitreous paint which runs and drips when fired, consequentially fine brush work would just run and blur together if the artist had taken the time to create fine line work. Interestingly, the bowl exteriors exhibit fine line work in white. The white kaolin paint does not run during firing.

DISTRIBUTION — The Woodburys report that the distribution for Kwakina Polychrome is in the area of the Zuni Reservation, east to El Moro, and south and west nearly to St. Johns, Arizona, and to the Petrified Forest National Monument (Woodbury/Woodbury 66). The abundance of Kwakina Polychrome at Raven Site Ruins extends this distribution well south of St. Johns, along the Upper Little Colorado River Drainage.

REMARKS — Kwakina Polychrome is very similar to Heshotauthla Polychrome in form and decoration, except that Kwakina Polychrome has the addition of the interior white slip in the case of bowls.

The addition of this white slip on the interior of bowls is an important development over a wide region of the Southwest. This is the first white interior slip in the Cibola region, and this application is also seen on the Showlow Polychromes to the west, and the Gila Polychromes to the south. The use of this white slip is a contemporaneous development shared by several groups of prehistoric people, who were producing several distinctly different ceramic types.

The addition of the white slip at Raven Site Ruins is largely due to the vitreous paint, which produced more brilliant colors when applied to a white slip rather than the previous red.

"KWAKINA NOT-QUITE-SO-POLYCHROME"

DATES — Temporal span of this very new ceramic "type" are the same as Kwakina Polychrome, i.e., A.D. 1325 to A.D. 1400.

REMARKS — Construction, form, painted design and distribution aspects of this new "type" are identical to Kwakina Polychrome with one important exception, there are no exterior white designs in the case of bowls.

We humorously call this variation of Kwakina Polychrome, "Kwakina Not-quite-so-polychrome" because vessels share all of the Kwakina Polychrome characteristics, except the use of white exterior paint in

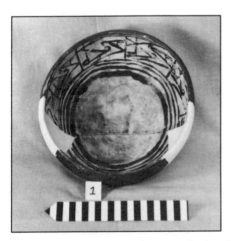 

Photo 15. "Kwakina Not-Quite-So-Polychrome". *Photos above show interior and exterior examples of "Kwakina Not-Quite-So-Polychrome". This variant, a recent discovery in the White Mountains, is identical to Kwakina Polychrome except that there is no use of the white exterior paint.*

the case of bowls. With the abundance of Kwakina Polychrome vessels discovered at Raven Site Ruins, sufficient examples exist to demonstrate some of the variations that the prehistoric potters used to create new designs.

"KWAKINA POLYCHROME-PLUS"

DATES — The temporal span of "Kwakina Polychrome-plus" are the same as for Kwakina Polychrome, A.D. 1325 to A.D. 1400.

REMARKS — Construction, form, painted design and distribution of "Kwakina Polychrome-plus" is identical in all respects to Kwakina Polychrome, except that on the interior of bowls there is the addition of a fugitive red paint in addition to the black glaze paint. Rinaldo reports the use of an additional red paint on the exterior of bowls which contrasts the red slip (Rinaldo 61). This could be a similar experiment. The fugitive red paint on the interior of bowls is in sharp contrast to the white slip.

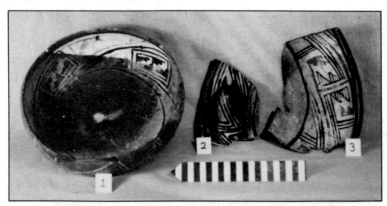

Photo 16. *"Kwakina Polychrome-plus" is identical to Kwakina Polychrome except that there is the addition of a red fugitive paint on the interior of bowls in addition to the glaze black. Several examples of this treatment have been excavated at Raven Site Ruins.*

"Kwakina Polychrome-plus" is identical in every way to Kwakina Polychrome except the prehistoric potters experimented with a red fugitive paint on the interior white slip in addition to the black glaze paint. Several new treatments with various paints have now been observed on the Kwakina Polychromes, kaolin white, vitreous black and now fugitive red were all combined and tried in various ways on the new white interior slip, and on the red-slipped exteriors.

"RAVEN POLYCHROME"

DATES — While we are pointing out the several ceramic variations that occurred with the introduction of a white slip on the interior of bowls between A.D. 1300 and A.D. 1400., it would be a good time to introduce a ceramic "type" that has been discovered at Raven Site Ruins. "Raven Polychrome" has been excavated at two locations at the site, both dating between A.D. 1300 and A.D. 1400.

"Raven Polychrome" shares characteristics with several of the ceramic types that we have discussed, but the design layouts, use of slips, and the pigments are very distinctive.

CONSTRUCTION — Vessels were made using the coil and scrape method. The body of the clay is light grey to buff. The temper is ground sherds, inclusions are angular.

Bowls are slipped red on the exterior. This red exterior slip ranges from a red-brown to orange. Exterior polish is of good quality, but polishing marks remain. The surface often appears slightly uneven.

The interior of bowls is slipped with white and red in zones of design. The white slip is applied first. This interior white slip is not a true white, but usually appears yellowish or buff. After areas of design are slipped white, the red slip is applied. Both slips are then polished together. Large areas of red slip cross over onto the white during the polishing and application of the red.

Black paint is then applied to the interior of bowls. This paint is not a glaze paint. It is matte, thin and often appears dull brown. No vitreous glaze paint was used on "Raven Polychromes".

White kaolin paint is then applied to the interior and the exterior of bowls. On the interior, to outline the black designs, and on the exterior to create unit motifs of thin line work, very similar to those found on late St. Johns Polychrome or Pinedale Polychrome vessels.

FORM — Only bowls and bowl fragments have been discovered at the site. Jars are rare with many of the ceramics of the period. Bowls are globular with in-curved rims. There is internal beveling at the rim and an external lip.

PAINTED DESIGNS — The interior of bowls display designs that were planned during the slip applications. The white slip was applied first in bold sweeping fields, followed by the application of a red slip on all of the remaining areas. Black painted designs were then applied with a thin, non-glaze paint which often appears matte and, even, brown. The black paint was used to create interlocked hachured and solid units in unison with the slip colors. The solid black units are then outlined with a thin line of white kaolin paint.

On the exterior of bowls we have excavated one complete vessel with unit designs in white kaolin paint, very similar to those seen on the

Photo 17. "Raven Polychrome" interior. *Yet another variation of the use of a white interior slip on bowls between A.D. 1300 and A.D. 1400. These vessels are very distinctive in design layout. The interiors employ both white and red slips. Interior motifs are hachured and solid units in a dull black paint used in combination with the slip applications. The solid units are then outlined in white kaolin paint. No glaze paint is used.*

Photo 17a. "Raven Polychrome" exterior. *White kaolin designs sometimes decorate the exterior in motifs which are similar to those found on Pinedale Polychrome or St. Johns Polychrome. The exterior is often unpainted.*

Pinedale Polychromes. Another bowl of the same type has been found with no exterior designs.

DISTRIBUTION — "Raven Polychrome" has been found in only two areas of Raven Site Ruins, both dating between A.D. 1300 and A.D. 1400. A large sherd of this same type has been discovered near the town of Springerville, Arizona which is located twelve miles south of Raven Site along the Upper Little Colorado River drainage.

REMARKS — "Raven Polychrome" demonstrates the extent of the experimentation that was happening between the years A.D. 1300 and A.D. 1400 with the use of white interior slips on bowls. When something new is excavated, the first step is to compare the vessel to all of the previously described types in the ceramic taxonomy. The only other recognized White Mountain Red Ware type which exhibits an increase in white interior slip use is Showlow Polychrome (see Showlow

Polychromes, page 50). Showlow Polychrome does not even resemble "Raven Polychrome". The Showlow Polychromes are a variant of the Fourmile Polychromes and they are very distinctive. The only resemblance between a Showlow Polychrome and a "Raven Polychrome" is the use of a white kaolin paint to outline the interior black motifs. "Raven Polychrome" resembles St. John's Polychrome only on the exterior of bowls. Both types exhibit white exterior linework executed in kaolin paint. One large sherd section of "Raven Polychrome" had no exterior paint whatsoever. The only other ceramic type in the White Mountains that uses an over-all white interior slip is Kwakina Polychrome. "Raven Polychromes" share no similarities with Kwakina Polychromes except that they both employ white interior slips. Kwakina Polychromes also employ glaze paints and "Raven Polychromes" do not.

I showed these "Raven Polychrome" specimens to several people who were attending the 1993 Ceramic Conference which was held in Flagstaff, Arizona. Everyone was quick to classify these ceramics as variants. Others suggested that "Raven Polychrome" was either Houck Ware or Querino Polychrome. The researchers who described Houck and Querino are listed in this volume (see *Synonyms to Ceramic Type Names,* page 151). Houck and Querino Polychromes share no similarities with "Raven Polychromes". Houck and Querino Polychromes are actually just Wingate Polychrome, exhibiting very wide white exterior paint, no white paint on the interior of bowls, etc. Quite frankly I don't know how anyone could even compare the two types, let alone mistake one for the other. If there existed in the White Mountain Archaeological Centers Collections only one example of "Raven Polychrome", it would probably be shelved as a variant, however, there are several examples of this type in the collections, and the designs and use of color are very distinctive.

PINNAWA GLAZE-ON-WHITE

DATES — Pinnawa Glaze-on-white is the next distinctive step in the use of overall white slips and glaze paint. This ceramic type dates between A.D. 1350 and A.D. 1450. Many examples have been discovered at Raven Site Ruins, most of these have been excavated from the south pueblo at the site. Only sherds in trash middens have been found in the earlier north pueblo area. The discovery of this late ceramic type in the north pueblo area (which was abandoned by A.D. 1380) gives weight to the argument that the south pueblo inhabitants were using the north pueblo empty rooms to deposit their trash. However, this ceramic type is found only in the extreme upper levels of the trash of the north pueblo. This is also the first ceramic type in the glazeware sequence produced after A.D. 1400, according to most of the literature.

With the ceramics that post-date A.D. 1400 we will see several form changes. The shape of bowls begin, at first, to have an increased incurvature at the rim, which increases the globular or rounded appearance of the shoulder, later developing into a sharp shoulder. The appearance of this sharp shoulder is more obvious on jars. The

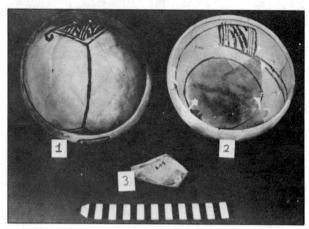

Photo 18. Pinnawa Glaze-on-white bowls and large sherd, *interior. The prehistoric potters now apply a thick white slip over the entire surface of the vessel. The vitreous black paint often melds with the white slip to produce greens, purples and even pinks. Example 1 displays large stylized birds on either side of the bowl interior.*

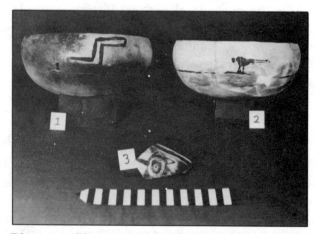

Photo 18a. Pinnawa Glaze-on-white bowls and large sherd, *exterior as shown in Photo 18. Example 2 has two birds, one on either side of the exterior of the vessel. The vitreous paint runs and blurs when it is fired, and life forms appear fuzzy and poorly executed. Example 3 is a large sherd painted with a bird's head.*

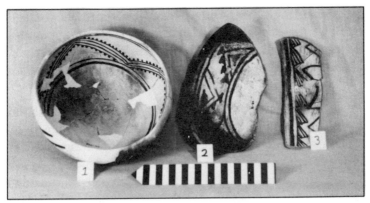

*Photo 18b. **Pinnawa Glaze-on-white bowl** and large glue-up sections, interior. On Example 2, the paint fired to a brilliant green.*

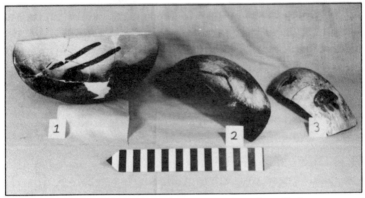

*Photo 18c. **Pinnawa Glaze-on-white bowl** and glue-up sections of Photo 18b showing the exterior.*

shoulders on jars later become very wide and flattened. These vessels appear almost "flying saucer" shaped, and they are very similar to the late Hopi Yellow Wares.

CONSTRUCTION — Vessels were produced using the coil and scrape method. The body of the clay is usually light grey, often becoming lighter colored toward the surface. The paste will sometimes appear pinkish-tan. These vessels rarely have a carbon streak. The temper is usually very fine with angular inclusions that appear white or grey.

The slip is usually a good white on the interior and exterior of bowls and on the exterior of jars. As we have seen in the development of the glaze wares, the prehistoric potters liked the results that were achieved by using the bright glaze paint on white surface, rather than on the earlier red slips. These vessels are now slipped totally in white. Martin and Rinaldo report that sometimes an area of the bowl toward the base will be left red and not slipped in white (Martin/Rinaldo 60). This is a transitional treatment from the Kwakina Polychromes to the use of the now overall white. Occasionally this white slip will appear yellowish-white, a cream is common, and grey is rare. The polish on these vessels is well-executed and smooth. Minor polishing marks are sometimes visible.

The paint is black glaze, and thick with a high luster. This paint often thins out at the edges of designs which changes the color to green and purple. The use of this thick black paint in conjunction with the white slip produces some interesting color changes and effects. It seems that the paint is penetrating the slip to produce purple-pinks and greenish-browns.

FORM — Woodbury and Woodbury report that jars predominate this ceramic type. They report that jars have globular bodies, low cylindrical necks, no sharp break in profile between neck and body, and a body diameter slightly greater than total height (Woodbury/Woodbury 66). No jars have yet been discovered at Raven Site Ruins, only bowls. Bowls have an in-curved rim, with no break in the curve. This in-curve is more pronounced than with earlier types, giving the body of the bowl a very globular shoulder. Bowl lips are usually rounded, sometimes showing an inward bevel. Bowl forms are very similar to Heshotauthla and Kwakina Polychromes.

PAINTED DESIGNS — Bowl exteriors usually have isolated design elements. Birds are a common motif from Raven Site Ruins. There are usually three of these units around the exterior of bowls. Simple geometric zigzags also occur. These units are similar to those found on the Pinedale Polychrome vessels which could be ownership marks or signatures.

Bowl interiors often have a broad band below the rim. The center of the vessel is often left undecorated. Between the band and the undecorated center a field of design is created around the internal body of the bowl. These interior designs are simple and quickly executed. Occasionally life forms, often birds, are found on the interior as well as the exterior of the vessel.

The brush work is often quick and careless, with banding lines varying in width and the ends of lines running across one another. The glaze paint often blurs the designs, giving them a sloppy appearance.

DISTRIBUTION — This type appears from El Morro, through the Zuni Reservation to the Puerco River. Also along the Little Colorado River to Cottonwood Wash. Pinnawa Glaze-on-white is very frequently found at Raven Site Ruins from the south pueblo area. These glaze wares have also been discovered at the recent excavations at

Rattlesnake Point Ruins in Lyman Lake State Park, six miles north of Raven Site Ruins.

REMARKS — Pinnawa Glaze-on-white is best distinguished from Kwakina Polychrome by the use of an overall white slip. Both types use the glaze paints. We have now observed the transition from red slips to red exterior and white interior, to overall white. The next type that we will examine, Kechipawan Polychrome, will still employ the overall white slip, but will add yet another splash of color.

The presence of Pinnawa Glaze-on-white in high frequencies confirms that the south pueblo areas of Raven Site Ruins was occupied long after A.D. 1400. The abandonment of this south pueblo area may mirror several northern abandonments in the Zuni areas when the Zuni people shifted their populations westward approximately forty miles to the historic "seven cities" including Hawikuh and the modern Zuni Pueblo.

WHITE-ON-RED POTTERY (UNNAMED)

DATES — This ceramic type is only briefly described and poorly researched. The Woodburys suggest that this ceramic type has shapes and designs similar to those found on late 14th century Zuni pottery, but add that the majority of these vessels are associated with other types found with Matsaki Polychrome, which probably was produced late in the 1400s and lasted until late in the 1700s. (Woodbury/ Woodbury 66). Bushnell feels that these white-on-red (unnamed) ceramics belong temporally near the time of transition from the white slipped glazed types, i.e., Kwakina Polychrome and Pinnawa Glaze-on-white, and Kechipawan, to the Matsaki Polychromes (Bushnell 55). The evidence from Raven Site Ruins confirms Bushnell's belief. These white-on-red (unnamed) ceramics are found in close association with the late Glaze-on-white ceramics in the south pueblo at Raven Site Ruins. They were produced from A.D. 1400 to possibly as late as A.D. 1475.

CONSTRUCTION — Vessels were made using the coil and scrape method. The body of the clay is light grey to buff. Temper is medium to fine, probably ground sherds.

Vessels are slipped with an overall red. This slip often appears red to orange. The polishing is well-executed and smooth, polishing marks are slightly visible. The only paint present on these vessels is a white kaolin on the exterior of both jars and bowls.

FORM — Jar forms are simple with globular bodies and vertical necks, very similar to the shapes of Pinnawa Glaze-on-white jars.

Bowls excavated from Hawikuh have simple profiles with the upper wall varying from vertical to inward sloping, as seen on most of the late glaze ware bowls from that site.

The bowl illustrated in Photo 19 from Raven Site Ruins, exhibits the angular profile and the presence of the sharp shoulder of the later Matsaki Polychromes.

PAINTED DESIGNS — The only paint present on this ceramic type is a chalky white kaolin which is found only on the exterior of bowls and

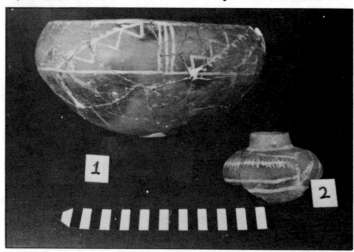

Photo 19. White-on-red pottery (unnamed). Insufficient examples of this ceramic type have been discovered for extensive research. The two examples shown are from the south pueblo at Raven Site Ruins. These specimens were found in association with several of the later glaze wares including Pinnawa Glaze-on-white and Kechipawan Polychrome, which suggests a date of production after A.D. 1400 and possibly as late as A.D. 1475.

the exterior of jars. A broad zone of design is created on the upper body of the bowls using simple, repeated, geometric elements. Pendants are common, as well as lines with intersecting cross bars.

Jars have similar patterns which are usually present on the upper body and sometimes the neck. These designs resemble those of polychrome Glaze-on-red vessels found at Hawikuh, which were made prior to the production of Matsaki Polychrome (Woodbury/Woodbury 66). This observation matches the evidence from Raven Site Ruins, where a long list of glaze wares are present including this unnamed type, but, to date, no Matsaki Polychromes have been excavated.

DISTRIBUTION — This white-on-red (unnamed) pottery has been discovered at Hawikuh & Kechipawan Ruins, and now southward at Raven Site Ruins, along the Upper Little Colorado River Drainage.

REMARKS — It is exciting to discover a ceramic type in the collections that barely exists in the literature. One must dig through a pile of dusty old reports and see if anyone has described any ceramics that are similar. This white-on-red pottery (unnamed) definitely belongs amongst the glaze wares even though it exhibits no glaze paint. It was produced during the same temporal period and the example illustrated in Photo 19 has the strong contrasting shoulder of the later Matsaki Polychromes. This form change is one of many that we will observe as we continue through these later ceramic sequences.

KECHIPAWAN POLYCHROME

DATES — This glaze ware ceramic type follows Pinnawa Glaze-on-white and is estimated to have produced between A.D. 1375 and A.D. 1475. This is the last glaze ware ceramic that was produced in the Zuni area and it marks the end of our glaze ware series.

Glaze wares did reappear later in the Zuni area in the form of the Hawikuh Polychromes (A.D. 1630 to A.D. 1680), these were probably stimulated by the Rio Grande Glaze Wares. To date, no Hawikuh Polychromes have been found at Raven Site Ruins. The latest habitation areas of the south pueblo are believed to have been abandoned shortly after A.D. 1500.

Following Kechipawan Polychrome, the glaze paint was abandoned and there was a dramatic shift in vessel shapes, colors, and designs. The ceramics that follow Kechipawan Polychrome temporally at Raven Site Ruins are the Matsaki types, i.e., Matsaki Polychrome and Matsaki Brown-on-buff. No Matsaki Polychromes have yet been excavated at Raven Site Ruins, however, several large ollas of the Matsaki Brown-on-buff variety have been found.

CONSTRUCTION — Vessels were made using the coil and scrape method. The body of the clay is usually light grey, becoming lighter toward the slipped surface. The temper is light colored and a medium to fine texture.

Vessels are slipped with an overall white, very similar to Pinnawa Glaze-on-white. Where the slip is thin it will sometimes appear pinkish. Some sherds of Kechipawan Polychrome from Table Rock Pueblo near St. Johns, Arizona, are reported to have a red surface on the lower part of bowls rather than the overall white (Martin/Rinaldo 60). These are probably a minor variation. No examples with this lower exterior red have been excavated from Raven Site Ruins.

The surface finish is usually well-executed and smooth. Minor polishing marks can sometimes be seen. There are basically two types of

Photo 20 & 20a. Kechipawan Polychrome bowl. *Interior 20 & exterior 20a. This ceramic type is the last glaze ware that was produced at Raven Site Ruins. Following this ceramic type, styles and pigments again changed. The red paint on these vessels is very similar to those we have observed on the variant type, "Kwakina Polychrome-plus".*

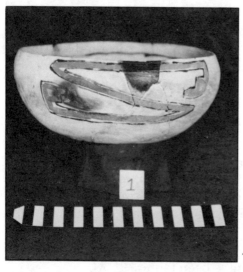

20a

paint found on Kechipawan Polychrome. The first is the black glaze paint which ranges from a good vitreous black to bright green. The glaze paint is applied with more control than the second color, a matte red. This red is very similar to the opaque fugitive red that we have observed on the variant type from Raven Site Ruins, "Kwakina Polychrome-plus".

FORM — Bowls are rounded with in-curved rims. The example illustrated in Photo 20 from Raven Site Ruins has a deep in-curve which tapers to a thin sharp lip. This lip is slightly thickened on the interior just below the rim. Vessel shapes are similar to Pinnawa Polychrome and the other white-slipped types of the 1300's and 1400's.

Jars have globular bodies and short necks. No examples of jars have been discovered, to date, from Raven Site Ruins.

PAINTED DESIGNS — Bowl interiors are decorated with designs in a broad band below the rim, over the entire interior, or centered in the bottom. These are usually quick and crude geometric designs, however the Woodburys report that life forms including stylized birds and occasionally human figures have been observed (Woodbury/Woodbury 66). Both the glaze paint and the matte red are used on the interior. The glaze paint is applied first, then the matte red is quickly applied as a filler to areas bordered in glaze.

Bowl exteriors usually display simple geometrics, sometimes isolated and without bordering lines, sometimes meandering around the entire upper body of the exterior of the bowl. The exterior sometimes is executed only in the glaze paint, but more often in both glaze and the matte red.

DISTRIBUTION — Kechipawan Polychrome is found from the El Morro and Ramah areas in New Mexico, through the Zuni area to the Petrified Forest and Leroux Wash. The discovery of Kechipawan Polychrome at Raven Site Ruins, extends this distribution to the south along the Upper Little Colorado River Drainage.

REMARKS — Kechipawan Polychrome is the last ceramic type in the glaze ware series. This began with Heshotauthla Polychrome with glaze paints being applied to red slips, through several experiments with white slips to bring out the glaze colors. The use of these white slips was being tried elsewhere in the Southwest at about the same time by several different groups, even those who were not using glaze paints.

The predominant ceramic type which temporally follows Kechipawan Polychrome is Matsaki Polychrome. Matsaki Polychrome is not a glaze ware. So far, excavations at Raven Site Ruins have not recovered any Matsaki Polychrome ceramics. However, several large ollas of Matsaki Brown-on-buff have been recovered from the same ceramic groups that contained Kechipawan Polychrome, Pinnawa Glaze-on-white, and very worn bowls of the Kwakina Polychrome variety.

MATSAKI BROWN-ON-BUFF

DATES — This ceramic type which has been abundantly excavated from the south pueblo at Raven Site Ruins, dates from A.D. 1475 to late in the 1600s (Woodbury/Woodbury 66). Other researchers estimate the dates of this ceramic type to be from A.D. 1400 to A.D. 1700 (Kintigh, personal communication). As of 1993, only eight rooms have so far been excavated in the south pueblo out of an estimated four hundred. So far, no Matsaki Polychrome has been found. Matsaki Polychrome and Matsaki Brown-on-buff are contemporaneous types, they were produced simultaneously on sites where they are found. As excavations at Raven Site Ruins continue, we will undoubtedly discover Matsaki Polychromes. What is fascinating about Matsaki Brown-on-buff, is that it represents a ceramic type that was still being produced long after Spanish contact in the Southwest. As we continue to excavate the south pueblo at Raven Site Ruins, with every stroke of the trowel, it is possible that we could un-earth evidence of Spanish contact at the site. At the very least, temporally, the site was occupied well into the 1500s.

CONSTRUCTION — Vessels were produced using the coil and scrape method. The body of the clay is predominantly light tan, occasionally light to dark grey, carbon streaks are common. The temper of the clay is medium texture with coarse particles. Inclusions are light grey, rounded quartz is often present, suggesting a sand rather than a sherd temper. No bowls of this type have been found to date at Raven Site Ruins, only jars. The Woodbury's report that the slips on bowls are similar to what we will discuss on jars (Woodbury/Woodbury 66).

The slip on jars from Raven Site Ruins is consistently cream to yellow, or white to cream. Vessels from Hawikuh are reported to be orange-buff, cream, and orange-tan. There seems to be a wide range of slip colors on this ceramic type, but the intent of the potter apparently is to produce a yellow or orange surface. According to modern Zuni color terminology; *"...mono-lingual Zunis do not distinguish at all between orange and yellow. The entire region is occupied by a single category."* (Lenneberg/Roberts 56).

Why were the prehistoric potters, around the year A.D. 1500, trying to produce a vessel that appeared yellow or orange? Sun worship?, a craving for citrus?, more likely an attempt to copy the Sikyatki ceramics from the north that were being produced by the proto-historic Hopi potters on Second Mesa. These excellent Yellow Wares from the north play a principle role in the development of the Katsina Cult, and were widely copied, possibly for this purpose, and if for no other reason, their beauty and symbolism. Following this theory, we will observe dramatic changes in vessel form that definitely copy the Hopi Style.

The polish and surface finish on the Matsaki Brown-on-buff vessels found at Raven Site Ruins begin with a poorly finished surface, crude with polishing marks present, and later proceed to be well polished and finely executed. This observation is consistent with the form changes that we will observe over the temporal span of the ceramic type. The Woodbury's report that the surfaces are always poorly finished, tool marks are present with striations that suggest the use of a stick rather than a stone (Woodbury/Woodbury 66). This very crude finish on

Treasures of Time Color Plates

(See detailed color plate captions immediately following
the color plate section.)

Plate 1. Puerco Black-on-red. A.D. 1000 to A.D. 1200.

Plate 2. Wingate Black-on-red. A.D. 1050 to A.D. 1200. Interior.

Plate 3. Wingate Black-on-red. A.D. 1050 to A.D. 1200. Exterior.

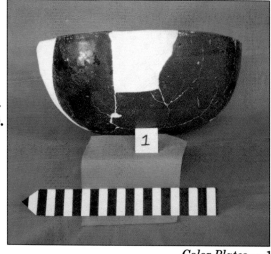

Plate 4. Wingate Polychrome. A.D. 1125 to A.D. 1200. Interior.

Plate 5. Wingate Polychrome. A.D. 1125 to A.D. 1200. Exterior.

Plate 6. St. Johns Black-on-red. A.D. 1175 to A.D. 1300.

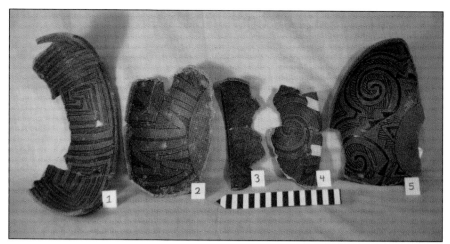

Plate 7. St. Johns Polychrome. A.D. 1175 to A.D. 1300. Interior.

Plate 8. St. Johns Polychrome. A.D. 1175 to A.D. 1300. Exterior.

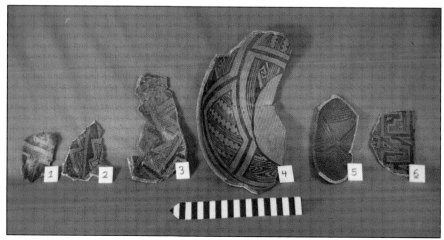

Plate 9. Springerville Polychrome. A.D. 1250 to A.D. 1300. Interior.

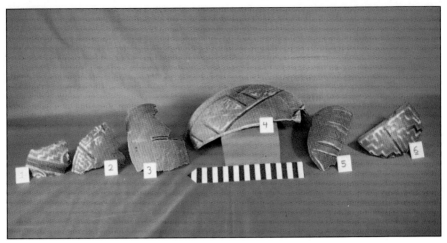

Plate 10. Springerville Polychrome. A.D. 1250 to A.D. 1300. Exterior.

Plate 11. Pinedale Black-on-red. A.D. 1275 to A.D. 1325.

Plate 12. Pinedale Polychrome. A.D. 1275 to A.D. 1325. Interior.

Plate 13. Pinedale Polychrome. A.D. 1275 to A.D. 1325. Exterior.

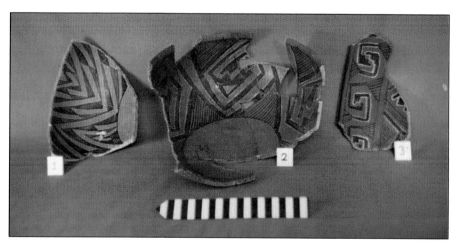

Plate 14. Cedar Creek Polychrome. A.D. 1300 to A.D. 1375.

Plate 15. Cedar Creek Polychrome. A.D. 1300 to A.D. 1375. Exteriors.

Plate 16. Fourmile Polychrome. A.D. 1325 to A.D. 1400. Interiors.

Plate 17. Fourmile Polychrome. A.D. 1325 to A.D. 1400. Exteriors.

Plate 18. Showlow Polychrome. A.D. 1325 to A.D. 1400.

Plate 19. Point of Pines Polychrome. A.D. 1400 to A.D. 1450. Interior.

Plate 20. Point of Pines Polychrome. A.D. 1400 to A.D. 1450. Exterior.

Plate 21. Heshotauthla Polychrome. A.D. 1300 to A.D. 1375/1400. Interior.

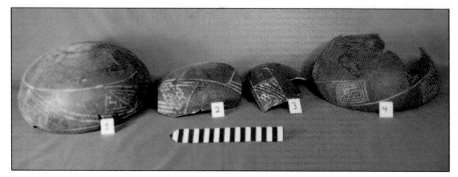

Plate 22. Heshotauthla Polychrome. A.D. 1300 to A.D. 1375/1400. Exterior.

Plate 23. Heshotauthla Polychrome Jars. A.D. 1300 to A.D. 1375/1400.

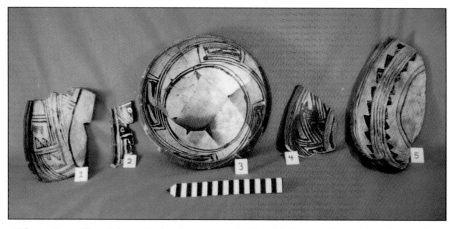

Plate 24. Kwakina Polychrome. A.D. 1325 to A.D. 1400. Interior.

Plate 25. Kwakina Polychrome. A.D. 1325 to A.D. 1400. Exterior.

Plate 26. "Raven Polychrome". A.D. 1300 to A.D. 1400.

Plate 27. Pinnawa Glaze-on-white. A.D. 1350 to A.D. 1450. Interior.

Plate 28. Pinnawa Glaze-on-white. A.D. 1350 to A.D. 1450. Exterior.

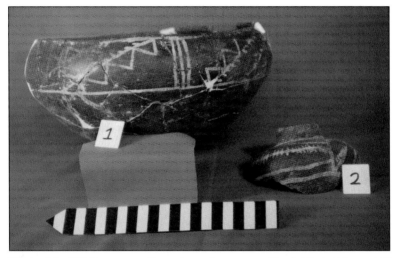

Plate 29. White-on-red pottery (unnamed). A.D. 1400 to A.D. 1475.

Plate 30. Kechipawan Polychrome. A.D. 1375 to A.D. 1475. Interior.

Plate 31. Kechipawan Polychrome. A.D. 1375 to A.D. 1475. Exterior.

Plate 32. Matsaki Brown-on-buff Ollas. A.D. 1400 to A.D. 1700.

Plate 33. Reserve Black-on-white. A.D. 900 to A.D. 1100.

Plate 34. Snowflake Black-on-white. A.D. 1100 to A.D. 1200.

Plate 35. Tularosa Black-on-white. A.D. 1200 to A.D. 1300.

Plate 36. Pinedale Black-on-white. A.D. 1275 to A.D. 1325.

Plate 37. Socorro Black-on-white. A.D. 950 to A.D. 1400.

Plate 38. Pinto Polychrome. A.D. 1150 to A. D. 1250.

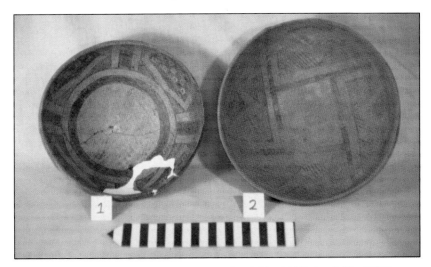

Plate 39. Pinto Black-on-red. A.D. 1150 to A.D. 1250.

Plate 40. Gila Polychrome. A.D. 1250 to A.D. 1400.

Plate 41. Tonto Polychrome. A.D. 1300 to A.D. 1400.

Plate 42. Heshotauthla Polychrome Clay Bodies and Tempers.

Plate 43. Fourmile Polychrome Clay Bodies and Tempers.

Plate 44. St. Johns Polychrome Clay Bodies and Tempers.

Plate 45. Tularosa Black-on-white Clay Bodies and Tempers.

Plate 46. Kwakina Polychrome Clay Bodies and Tempers.

Plate 47. Tonto Polychrome, Room 31, Raven Site Ruins.

Plate 48. Tonto Polychrome Olla.

Treasures of Time

Color Plate Captions

Plate 1. Puerco Black-on-red. A.D. 1000 to A.D. 1200. Bowls often have very vertical sides as seen in Examples 1 and 4. The very Grecian looking scrolls as seen in Examples 2 and 3 are also common. This is the first red ware to appear in the Upper Little Colorado Region.

Plate 2. Wingate Black-on-red. A.D. 1050 to A.D. 1200. Interior. The black paint often appears fuzzy or blurred. Bowl bottoms are often left undecorated. The hachured units are usually larger than the solid black units.

Plate 3. Wingate Black-on-red. A.D. 1050 to A.D. 1200. Exterior. The small black design unit seen between the two restored plaster areas of the bowl could represent a signature unit. These signature units are rare on other ceramic types, but not uncommon on Wingate Black-on-red.

Plate 4. Wingate Polychrome. A.D. 1125 to A.D. 1200. Interior. Some Wingate Polychromes exhibiting the Tularosa Style may have been produced as late as A.D. 1300. The bottoms of bowls are usually left undecorated. The black paint ranges from a good mineral black to a dull brown. Examples 2 and 3 exhibit the dull brown paint that is not unusual. The hachured units are still slightly larger than the solid units. This is the first polychrome pottery to appear in the White Mountains.

Plate 5. Wingate Polychrome. A.D. 1125 to A.D. 1200. Exterior. The addition of the wide white exterior designs create the first polychrome of the Upper Little Colorado Region. After these early experiments with wide white and red exterior slips, the exterior white designs become narrower and narrower and they are painted on an overall red slipped exterior.

Plate 6. St. Johns Black-on-red. A.D. 1175 to A.D. 1300. There are no exterior designs exhibited on this ceramic type. Bowl bottoms are usually left undecorated. Designs are executed either in Wingate Style or more usually Tularosa Style. Interlocked solid and hachured spirals are very common.

Plate 7. St. Johns Polychrome. A.D. 1175 to A.D. 1300. Interior. Interior designs are very similar to St. Johns Black-on-red. Hachuring is still slightly larger than the solid units. Example 5 shows the use of a black glaze paint diagnostic on Heshotauthla Polychrome, but not uncommon on the later St. Johns Polychromes.

Plate 8. St. Johns Polychrome. A.D. 1175 to A.D. 1300. Exterior. The exterior white paint is the key to distinguishing St. Johns Polychrome from Wingate Polychrome. The white designs are narrower and there is a distinctive transition from the early St. Johns Polychromes with wider white exterior designs, to the later St. Johns Polychromes with narrow and narrower exterior white line work. Notice that Example 5 has the narrowest white line work. Example 5 also has the late black glaze paint on the interior of the bowl section.

Plate 9. Springerville Polychrome. A.D. 1250 to A.D. 1300. Interior. Springerville Polychrome is a variant of St. Johns Polychrome and splitting Springerville Polychrome as a separate type may be erroneous. Raven Site Ruins is located at the very center of the core area of production for Springerville Polychrome and very few examples have been found. Example 4 is probably a Heshotauthla Polychrome demonstrating the classic Pinedale Style and not a Springerville Polychrome.

Plate 10. Springerville Polychrome. A.D. 1250 to A.D. 1300. Exterior. Springerville Polychrome is probably not a distinctive type, at best it is simply a variant of St. Johns Polychrome. The addition of small amounts of black paint on the exterior along with the standard white exterior paint distinguishes Springerville Polychrome from St. Johns Polychrome. Examples 1, 2, and 6 are classic St. Johns Polychrome with the addition of some black exterior paint. Example 4 is probably a Heshotauthla Polychrome also with the addition of the exterior black paint.

Plate 11. Pinedale Black-on-red. A.D. 1275 to A.D. 1325. Pinedale ceramics and the years following A.D. 1300 ushered the Katsina Cult into the White Mountains of Arizona. Technological advances in ceramic technique and social/cultural changes are mirrored in the designs found on the pottery beginning with the Pinedale ceramic types. Pinedale design units are isolated, sometimes singular on the exteriors of bowls and jars. They occasionally resemble the signature elements as found on Wingate Black-on-red. The Pinedale style is distinctive, bold, and a dramatic shift from earlier ceramic designs.

Plate 12. Pinedale Polychrome. A.D. 1275 to A.D. 1325. Interior. Examples 2 and 4 exhibit the Pinedale "squiggle" design element which is diagnostic to the type. Black and white designs can be found on the interiors of bowls, or just black-on-red. Example 3 could be a Cedar Creek Polychrome and not a Pinedale Polychrome, the use of the thin white border around the black design elements is more typical of the Cedar Creek Polychromes.

Plate 13. Pinedale Polychrome. A.D. 1275 to A.D. 1325. Exterior. The exterior design elements can be white or black and white. They are usually isolated and widely spaced around the vessel. Notice how narrow the white exterior lines are compared to the earlier St. Johns Polychrome examples. Example 5 exhibits the continuous upper rim band which is common.

Plate 14. Cedar Creek Polychrome. A.D. 1300 to A.D. 1375. Interiors can be either black on red or black and white on red. The use of white to outline the black designs is a common treatment. Most examples from Raven Site exhibit an orange slip.

Plate 15. Cedar Creek Polychrome. A.D. 1300 to A.D. 1375. Exteriors. The white is commonly used to outline the black designs. The unit elements that were observed on Pinedale Black-on-red and Pinedale Polychrome now elongate and begin to encompass a zone of design around the entire vessel. Example 2 exhibits a sprouting corn glyph.

Plate 16. Fourmile Polychrome. A.D. 1325 to A.D. 1400. Interiors. This very distinctive ceramic type can be quickly identified by the rich red slip, black bands and design units outlined in white and the lack of symmetry. The Fourmile Polychromes reflect the development of the Katsina Cult at Raven Site Ruins after A.D. 1325. Many of the designs depict Katsina themes.

Plate 17. Fourmile Polychrome. A.D. 1325 to A.D. 1400. Exteriors. Black rim bands outlined in white followed by a second lower band which creates a continuous design field are diagnostic of the type. Interlocked "F" hooks are a common motif.

Plate 18. Showlow Polychrome. A.D. 1325 to A.D. 1400. Showlow Polychrome would best be described as a variant of Fourmile Polychrome. The only difference between the two types is a slight increase in the use of white slip on the upper regions of jars in the case of the Showlow Polychromes. Example 2 was re-discovered by the author at a yard sale in Ohio in 1985, for five dollars. The vessel is signed by J. W. Fewkes. It is now on loan from the White Mountain Archaeological Center to the visitors center at Homolovi Ruins near Winslow Arizona, where it was originally excavated.

Plate 19. Point of Pines Polychrome. A.D. 1400 to A.D. 1450. Interior. This ceramic type is a poor copy of the Fourmile Polychromes. The vessels were produced by potters who were not familiar with polychrome ceramic technologies.

Plate 20. Point of Pines Polychrome. A.D. 1400 to A.D. 1450. Exterior. Point of Pines Polychrome is best described as a degenerate Fourmile. These later potters attempted to produce a similar ceramic type and they copied the design motifs including the black banding outlined in white, but these attempts fall far short of the Fourmile ceramic technologies.

Plate 21. Heshotauthla Polychrome. A.D. 1300 to A.D. 1375/1400. Interior. Heshotauthla commonly displays the Pinedale Style. Shiny black, glassy, vitreous paint with dense designs are common. This ceramic type begins a new ceramic tradition at Raven Site Ruins. The vitreous paint runs and blurs during firing, however, these new glazes can produce greens and even purple colors. One group of potters split from the White Mountain Red Ware tradition and opted to use the new glazes and new colors. This new ceramic tradition begins with Heshotauthla Polychrome and later becomes the Zuni Glaze Ware sequence which survives well into the 1400's.

Plate 22. Heshotauthla Polychrome. A.D. 1300 to A.D. 1375/1400. Exterior. Fine thin exterior lines with unit elements often linked by additional thin line work are typical. The exterior white kaolin paint does not run like the black vitreous interior paint, making the fine line work possible. This fine white exterior line work is a continuation from the wide white slip used on Wingate Polychrome exteriors then the thinner line work found on St. John Polychrome, and now continuing with the very fine exterior white lines as shown.

Plate 23. Heshotauthla Polychrome Jars. A.D. 1300 to A.D. 1375/ 1400. Very few jars of any ceramic type are found at Raven Site Ruins between the years A.D. 1300 to A.D. 1400. Tularosa jars dating between A.D. 1200 and A.D. 1300 are very abundant at the site. After A.D. 1300 the Tularosa Black-on-white jars are re-used for nearly 100 years until the appearance of Matsaki Brown-on-buff ceramic jars after A.D. 1400.

Plate 24. Kwakina Polychrome. A.D. 1325 to A.D. 1400. Interior. The white slip over the entire interior of the bowl is the key to distinguishing this ceramic type from Heshotauthla Polychrome. The black vitreous glaze paint when applied to a white surface blends with the slip to create greens and even purples during firing. Examples 1 and 4 also exhibit a fugitive red paint.

Plate 25. Kwakina Polychrome. A.D. 1325 to A.D. 1400. Exterior. This ceramic type may have been produced after A.D. 1400. The exterior of this ceramic type is very similar to Heshotauthla Polychrome, with the fine white line work often in units and often linked by lines of equal width.

Plate 26. "Raven Polychrome". A.D. 1300 to A.D. 1400. This new ceramic type always has wide white areas of slip on the interior of bowls. The use of hachured and solid right triangles are a common motif. The exterior of bowls can be unpainted or decorated with white kaolin lines similar in width to those found on later St. Johns Polychrome vessels.

Plate 27. Pinnawa Glaze-on-white. A.D. 1350 to A.D. 1450. Interior. These bowls are slipped totally in white, interior and exterior. Vitreous glaze paint is used to create very simple designs. Remnants of the Pinedale Style can still be seen. Bowl rims now begin to curve in more sharply.

Plate 28. Pinnawa Glaze-on-white. A.D. 1350 to A.D. 1450. Exterior. Example 2 exhibits a bird icon and Example 3 possibly a bear paw. Exterior design elements are often isolated resembling the units found on Pinedale Polychromes, except that they are much less complex.

Plate 29. White-on-red Pottery (un-named). A.D. 1400 to A.D. 1475. The extreme in-curve of the rim of the bowl is a form change apparent on several ceramic types that were produced after A.D. 1450. Increased contact from the south, below the Mogollon Rim, occurred at Raven Site during this time. These form changes may have been influenced by increased contact with the Salado Cultural areas.

Plate 30. Kechipawan Polychrome. A.D. 1375 to A.D. 1475. Interior. This ceramic type marks the end of the Glaze ware series which began in A.D. 1300 with Heshotauthla Polychrome. These bowls have sharply in-curved rims similar to Pinnawa Glaze-on-white. Green glaze paint is common. Designs by this time have deteriorated in detail and have been replaced with bold brush strokes of glaze color.

Plate 31. Kechipawan Polychrome. A.D. 1375 to A.D. 1475. Exterior. Designs are still unit in nature as seen on the earlier glaze wares in this series.

Plate 32. Matsaki Brown-on-buff Ollas. A.D. 1400 to A.D. 1700. Several of these ollas have been found in the south pueblo area of Raven Site Ruins. This ceramic type may be an attempt to copy the northern Hopi Yellow Wares. This is evident by the wide shoulder area in Example 2 which is very similar to the northern forms. The buff color is often yellowish. These form and color changes are associated with the development and expansion of the Katsina Cult.

Plate 33. Reserve Black-on-white. A.D. 900 to A.D. 1100. Early Cibola White Ware. Hachuring usually contrasts the element it fills. Examples 2, 4, and 6 are sherds showing the exterior of bowls with white slip finger dots and stripes. This exterior white slip treatment occurred at A.D. 1100.

Plate 34. Snowflake Black-on-white. A.D. 1100 to A.D. 1200. Simple solid elements predominate. Checkerboards are common as are vertical lines on the necks of ollas. This ceramic type has been a "catch-all" category for many black-on-white ceramics that are difficult to classify.

Plate 35. Tularosa Black-on-white. A.D. 1200 to A.D. 1300. At Raven Site Ruins Tularosa Black-on-white is found in great abundance with St. Johns Polychrome in the north pueblo. Interlocked spirals, hachured and solid are common. Example 3 exhibits a spirit break in the band around the neck of the olla. Jars and dippers are the most common form, bowls are rare.

Plate 36. Pinedale Black-on-white. A.D. 1275 to A.D. 1325. This ceramic type along with Tularosa Black-on-white are the latest Cibola White Wares found at Raven Site. Shortly after A.D. 1300, Black-on-white ceramics disappear entirely and are replaced by glaze wares and polychromes.

Plate 37. Socorro Black-on-white. A.D. 950 to A.D. 1400. The temporal range of this Cibola White Ware makes it less useful as a dating aid during excavations than many other ceramic types. Designs are wide, bold, eclectic. The example shown above is an olla, and the neck has been completely worn away from the repeated placement and replacement of a stone lid over many years of use.

38. Pinto Polychrome. A.D. 1150 to A.D. 1250. This ceramic type was traded to Raven Site from the south. Bowls are easy to recognize. Hachured units are larger than the solid units and the bottom of bowls is left as an undecorated circle, square, or triangle. The exterior is red slipped and unpainted.

Plate 39. Pinto Black-on-red. A.D. 1150 to A.D. 1250. Designs are the same as Pinto Polychrome. Pinto Black-on-red lacks the interior white slip that is employed in the construction of Pinto Polychrome.

Plate 40. Gila Polychrome. A.D. 1250 to A.D. 1400. This type developed out of Pinto Polychrome and was widely traded in the prehistoric Southwest. Examples that have been discovered at Raven Site were traded from the south, well below the Mogollon Rim. Bowl rims are often flared and decorated with wavy lines. Spirit breaks are common. The entire interior of the bowl is decorated. These vessels often lack symmetry.

Plate 41. Tonto Polychrome. A.D. 1300 to A.D. 1400. This type developed out of the Pinto-Gila Polychrome sequence. Many researchers feel that this type was produced well after A.D. 1400.

Plate 42. Heshotauthla Polychrome Clay Bodies and Tempers. The Heshotauthla Polychrome examples from Raven Site Ruins often display a very dark grey or even black clay body. Ground sherds are usually used for temper which appear as angular inclusions. These inclusions often appear as light grey or even white, contrasting the paste.

Plate 43. Fourmile Polychrome Clay Bodies and Tempers. The Fourmile Polychrome examples from Raven Site Ruins usually display a tan or light buff clay body. The rich red slip on the interior and exterior surfaces intrudes into the clay body and can easily be seen in profile. The temper is finely ground sherds and the inclusions are white, red or even black, but these are difficult to see with the naked eye.

Plate 44. St. Johns Polychrome Clay Bodies and Tempers. The St. Johns Polychrome examples that have been discovered at Raven Site Ruins have clay bodies of several colors. It is not unusual to find tan, grey, buff, white, yellow, pink and even black. The darker clay bodies such as very dark grey and black may be the result of using scoria sand as a temper. Ground sherds are usually used for temper.

Plate 45. Tularosa Black-on-white Clay Bodies and Tempers. The Tularosa Black-on-white examples from Raven Site Ruins display a very consistent coloring throughout the clay body. The majority of the examples are light grey. Only occasionally will a vessel be discovered with a dark grey paste, and very rarely a yellow clay body. The temper is finely ground sherds and inclusions are angular, very small and difficult to see without magnification.

Plate 46. Kwakina Polychrome Clay Bodies and Tempers. The Zuni Glaze Wares found at Raven Site Ruins often display a dark grey or black clay body. The white interior and red exterior slips are visible in profile and they do penetrate the paste. The temper is angular and medium to fine in texture.

Plate 47. Tonto Polychrome, Room 31, Raven Site Ruins. Archaeologist Jeff Brown dusts a Tonto Polychrome olla in situ. The earth from within the jar was retained for floatation.

Plate 48. Tonto Polychrome Olla. This large olla from room 31 in the south pueblo of Raven Site Ruins at first appeared to be a Tonto Polychrome jar that had been traded from the south to Raven Site Ruins. Petro-analysis revealed that the vessel was actually produced at Raven Site. This prehistoric copy is of a much higher quality than the Tonto Polychrome originals that were produced by the Salado Culture below the Mogollon Rim.

vessels has not been observed on the Raven Site Ruins examples, not even on those that were produced early in the temporal span of this type. The paint used on Matsaki Brown-on-buff is a chocolate brown matte. It appears darker, blacker, on the surfaces where it has been thickly applied, and lighter, browner on thinner applications.

FORM — When discussing this ceramic type, form changes are critical. Two things are happening that fall into the temporal span of this type and the sister type Matsaki Polychrome.

First, the prehistoric potters are trying to copy the Hopi Yellow Wares from the north, which were widely traded and highly prized. This attempt at copying these wares is probably related to the development of the Katsina Cult.

The second confusion is that this type survived and was produced after Spanish contact, which means that the potters were also copying the vessels that the Spanish introduced. I could spend the next five or six pages describing the form variations that have been observed during the temporal span of these ceramic types. But now we are bumping into history and leaving prehistory. Naturally the potters copied the tea pots and coffee cups that the Spanish brought. The Woodbury's report that these multiple form changes could mean that Matsaki Brown-on-buff was produced more commonly during the post-contact period (Woodbury/Woodbury 66). I hope that they are right. If they are, then it is possible that we will excavate a Spanish visor, horseshoe, or lance at Raven Site Ruins. But remember, there are two variables for the form changes, Spanish contact and the mimicry of the Hopi Yellow Wares. Most of the evidence that we have observed at Raven Site Ruins, indicates that the potters were attempting to copy the fine ceramics that were being traded from the north. This desire to have similar ceramics is very likely tied to the development of the Katsina Cult in the Upper Little Colorado Region.

The basic form changes that we have observed, from the vessels excavated at Raven Site Ruins to date, indicate a shift from a globular-bodied jar early in the development of the type (remember that no bowls of this type have yet been discovered at the site) to an angular shoulder, and then to a very wide shoulder that spans out from the neck and mouth of the jar and curves sharply toward the bottom creating a "flying saucer" shaped vessel. These later forms are clearly copies of the Hopi Yellow Wares. No copies that mimic the Spanish contact materials have yet been discovered. This could indicate that Raven Site Ruins was abandoned before Spanish contact, just after A.D. 1500, or that we have not yet excavated in the right place to find these Spanish contact copies.

PAINTED DESIGNS — The jar exteriors from Raven Site Ruins are decorated over the entire vessel, from the lip to very near the base with a matte brown paint. Most of the jars in the White Mountain Archaeological Centers Collections were excavated from the same area of the south pueblo, in fact, the same contiguous room block. These exhibit several cloud motifs, including a right triangle with a flight icon, over mountains over earth-land. A unilateral terrace with an

Photo 21. Matsaki Brown-on-buff ollas. *Notice the form change from a very globular jar, to a sharp shoulder, and later, to a wide rounded shoulder that quickly tapers to the vessel bottom creating a "flying saucer" shape, see Photo 21a, Example 2. This results in a vessel with a large area between the shoulder and the neck, mimicking the Hopi Yellow Wares that were traded from the north.*

Photo 21a. Matsaki Brown-on-buff ollas. *Example 1 exhibits two large drilled holes on either side, possibly used to hang the olla, or create a handle of other perishable material that did not survive preservation.*

extension, another cloud symbol is also present. These are combined with icons that represent "house". The ollas that exhibit these combinations of "cloud/house" are representing the phratral organization "Patki" (see *Symbols*, page 139). Other vessels of this type have a "rattlesnake" pattern, i.e., diamonds linked at the ends which contain wavy squiggles inside. None of these ollas are symmetrical in design. Some patterns are repeated but different patterns and symbols will appear only on one area of the olla, disregarding the majority of the design layout.

Banding is employed, usually above the shoulder of the olla, creating an undecorated, or minimally decorated, area between the shoulder and the neck of the vessel. The neck of the olla is decorated. The body of the vessel displays another banding line low on the body, separating the undecorated bottom of the vessel from the painted areas which cover the surface with tightly packed designs.

DISTRIBUTION — The Matsaki vessels, both the Polychromes and the Brown-on-buff varieties, were discovered at Hawikuh and Kechipawan Ruins in 1953. These types were believed to be isolated to six historic Zuni towns all within a twelve-mile radius of modern Zuni. The discovery of Matsaki Brown-on-buff in large quantities at Raven Site Ruins, which lies almost a hundred miles south of the Zuni area, increases the distribution of at least the Brown-on-buff ceramic type, well to the south of the core area.

REMARKS — The presence of Matsaki Brown-on-buff in large quantities at Raven Site Ruins, presents many questions. This ceramic type is found in association with very worn, well used, Kwakina Polychrome bowl fragments that were used as scoops near mealing bins after the original bowls were broken. Pinnawa Glaze-on-white and Kechipawan Polychrome bowls of good condition are also found in association with the Matsaki material. All of these ceramic types are believed to have been produced certainly late in the 1400s, and possibly after A.D. 1500. This ceramic evidence suggests that the south pueblo at Raven Site Ruins was occupied until about A.D. 1500 and possibly later.

The form changes from a globular-bodied jar, to one with a wide shoulder that tapers quickly to the bottom of the olla are an attempt to copy the Hopi Yellow Wares which were produced to the north of the site. The attempt to produce a more yellow slip similarly copies these northern types. These form and color changes are associated with the development and expansion of the Katsina Cult during this time.

Chapter 6

The Cibola White Wares
of Raven Site Ruins

We will now boldly go where no one has gone before...into the taxonomical abyss of the ceramic group called the Cibola White Wares. These ceramic types have been split and re-split, named, described, and re-named and re-defined so many times that many people who have attempted their doctoral thesis on this subject have been straight-jacketed and carted away never to be seen again. If you thought the White Mountain Red Ware differentiations were confusing, I suggest that you do not read this section, just look at the pictures, they are sufficiently confusing by themselves.

The Cibola White Wares are a difficult group of ceramic types to differentiate, especially if only sherds are available for examination. These black-on-white types share very similar characteristics in form, temper, clay bodies, and paint. The differentiations are made by comparing the designs on the vessels and many of these are nearly the same.

We will examine only those Cibola White Wares that have been discovered at Raven Site Ruins. I will do my very best to point out similarities and differences as we proceed through time, ceramic type to ceramic type. Don't blame me if they all look alike, I didn't name them, or split them, but we must live with the taxonomical monster that is roaming the literature.

The black-on-white ceramic types were produced from about A.D.850 to around A.D. 1250. Remember that the Cibola White Wares are only one group of several white ware groups that have regionally been defined. The Cibola White Wares fall well into this temporal span, the only exception that we have observed at Raven Site Ruins is the presence of Tularosa Black-on-white which was produced at least until A.D. 1300. After A.D. 1300, the black-on-white ceramics died out and were replaced by the more desirable polychromes.

The Cibola White Wares share several common attributes that help define them from other white wares. The black paint on these white slipped ceramics has a mineral rather than a carbon base. The body of the clay, or paste, is light or dark grey, sometimes white. Early in the Cibola White Ware ceramic production, a sand temper was used, but by A.D. 875 this was replaced with a ground sherd temper. All of the Cibola White Ware types that we have discovered to date from Raven Site Ruins were produced after A.D. 875 and all of the individual types that we will examine use a ground sherd temper.

The early white slips on these ceramics was thin and poorly polished. With many of the earlier types, only one surface, in the case of bowls, is slipped, and jars are often only partially slipped. Often angular inclusions of the temper show through the surface polish of the vessel. After about A.D. 950, the slips and polish of the Cibola White Wares greatly improves, and between A.D. 1100 and A.D. 1300 a good thick slip and high polish was finally achieved.

There is a lot of debate in the literature about where the Cibola White Wares were actually produced. Variations in temper and paint composition suggest localized manufacture. At Raven Site Ruins, beginning around the year A.D.1200, at the very end of the Snowflake Black-on-white ceramic production, and the beginning of the appearance of Tularosa Black-on-white, ollas were locally produced in large quantities. This is evident by the abundance of Tularosa material that has been excavated and proven by the example shown in photo 22. This olla "slumped" during the firing process, and was discarded. It was excavated from a trash midden in the north pueblo area. The presence of rejects from the ceramic production process are good evidence of local manufacture.

Photo 22. A "slumped" Snowflake/Tularosa Black-on-white olla. *This vessel was locally produced at Raven Site Ruins at approximately A.D. 1200. Snowflake and Tularosa varieties are difficult to differentiate. This example is probably a late Snowflake and is good evidence of production of the Cibola White Wares at the site. It was discarded after a miscalculated firing.*

Tremendous quantities of Tularosa material have been discovered at the site in association with St. Johns Polychrome ceramics. The St. Johns material was widely traded throughout the Southwest, and it is also excavated in large quantities at Raven Site Ruins. It is very probable that the potters at the site were producing large amounts of both of these ceramic types to trade out. This could account for the appearance of at least this phase of the Cibola White Ware ceramics at other sites in the area where local manufacture is questionable.

The Cibola White Wares are very difficult to differentiate, especially when only sherds are available for analysis. Fortunately, being a lumper myself, I have observed only four different Cibola White Wares in the White Mountain Archaeological Centers Collections. I'm sure that if a proficient splitter examined the collections that they would easily point out a dozen or so new types that I personally can not distinguish.

The five types that we will examine are; Reserve Black-on-white, Snowflake Black-on-white, Tularosa Black-on-white, Pinedale Black-on-white and Socorro Black-on-white.

RESERVE BLACK-ON-WHITE

DATES — Reserve Black-on-white probably appeared around the year A.D.900 and was produced until just after A.D. 1100. It overlaps temporally with Snowflake Black-on-white, the next Cibola White Ware in the sequence. We find Reserve Black-on-white in the deepest excavation levels so far achieved in the north pueblo areas at Raven Site Ruins.

CONSTRUCTION — Vessels were made using the coil and scrape method. The paste is usually light grey, sometimes dark grey, and rarely tan. A carbon streak is sometimes present. The temper of the clay is coarse to medium, inclusions are light grey and angular.

The slip is a good white when well-preserved. On vessels that exhibit heavy use the slip is often worn away and thinned and will appear more grey than white. Bowls are slipped on the interior only, or on the interior and the exterior but the exterior slip is thin and poorly polished. Often the exterior is left un-slipped and the clay body is poorly polished. Often angular fragments of the temper show through the polish. The use of a well-polished slip only on the interior of bowls we have observed before, on the contemporaneous type Puerco Black-on-red. Puerco Black-on-red vessels are slipped on the exterior, but this slip is thin and barely polished. Both of these types have designs on the interior only. The white slip is the canvas, the surface where the artist creates her designs. This use of the interior slip only is also found on another contemporaneous type south and east of Raven Site Ruins. The Mimbres vessels with their often whimsical designs use only the interior of bowls as the design surface and the exteriors are left poorly finished. This seemed to be the standard ceramic method between A.D. 900 and A.D. 1100.

The paint is a good black, it rarely appears brown or brown-black. The vessels were fired in an oxygen-reduced atmosphere which results in this good black paint. If air enters the firing, the black paint will become reddish. Few examples exhibit this error in firing. Fire clouds are common.

FORM — Most of the examples of Reserve Black-on-white from Raven Site Ruins are in the form of bowls. This is probably because it is very difficult to distinguish one black-on-white type from another, especially if only sherds are available for analysis. Sherds of Reserve Black-on-white jars probably exist in the collections, but until a good splitter spends an afternoon in the lab, we will simply describe the bowls.

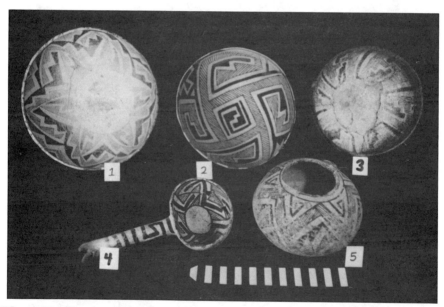

Photo 23. Reserve Black-on-white. Designs are simple, hachuring usually contrasts the element which it fills, but not always. Line work is very well executed but not as fine as later Cibola White Wares. Examples 1 and 3 show heavy wear. The dipper is a late Reserve Black-on-white, showing similarities to Tularosa Black-on-white. The jar shown in Example 5 demonstrates very heavy wear, the neck is completely worn away. This jar could be typed as Snowflake Black-on-white.

Bowls have very vertical sides, sometimes almost flaring. They have a small, sometimes slightly flattened bottom, from which the bowl body widens toward the lip. Rims are never in-curved. The body of the bowl narrows to the lip. Lips are thin, sometimes almost sharp, and occasionally slightly rounded. These bowls often have very thin construction, one example from Raven Site Ruins has a body thickness of no more than three millimeters.

PAINTED DESIGNS — Bowl interiors usually have an undecorated bottom defined by a circle. The designs extend from this circle up to the rim. There are usually no upper banding lines on bowls. The edge of the rim is often ticked with wide units. Designs include solid and

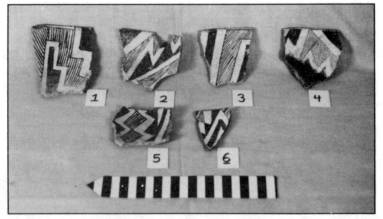

Photo 23a. Reserve Black-on-white sherds, interior of bowls. These are difficult to differentiate from Snowflake Black-on-white.

Photo 23b. Reserve Black-on-white sherds, exterior of bowls shown in Photo 23a, with white slip used to create dabbed designs. This occurred at A.D. 1100. This treatment is very similar to Wingate Polychrome, which appears at exactly the same time.

hachured motifs with an unpainted area between. The hachuring often opposes the element that it fills, but not always. These interlocked hachured and solid units could best be described as Wingate Style. Line work is often very well-executed, but not as fine as in later black-on-white types. There is more open space that is left unpainted, and the line widths are nearly the same.

DISTRIBUTION — Reserve Black-on-white is found from the Reserve, New Mexico area, north to the Puerco River, and west to Snowflake, Arizona, and as far south as the Mogollon Rim. It is the predominant black-on-white type at Raven Site Ruins for the temporal period between A.D. 900 until A.D. 1100. As you move west out of the Raven Site Ruins area toward Snowflake, less of this ceramic type is encountered, and more of the semi-contemporaneous type, i.e., Snowflake Black-on-white is found (Martin/Rinaldo/Longacre 61).

REMARKS — Reserve Black-on-white is one of the earliest known ceramics from Raven Site Ruins. It is discovered in the deepest excavations to date in the area of the north pueblo. As with most of the Cibola White Wares, it is very difficult to distinguish one type from another using only sherds, unless the sherd is from an area of the vessels that give the researcher other clues, such as the thin tapered rim of the bowl.

One important design element to recognize about Reserve Black-on-white ceramics, is the use of the exterior white slip designs, on an otherwise un-slipped surface at A.D.1100, in the case of bowls. This is a very similar application of the first use of exterior slips as we have seen on the Wingate Polychromes which are contemporaneous to Reserve Black-on-white. Reserve Black-on-white was disappearing at A.D.1100, and Wingate Polychrome was being introduced.

SNOWFLAKE BLACK-ON-WHITE

DATES — Snowflake Black-on-white was produced from A.D. 1100 to around A.D. 1200 when the type was replaced by Tularosa Black-on-white. Snowflake follows the Reserve Black-on-white ceramics in the temporal sequence. Dittert/Plog give Snowflake Black-on-white a wider temporal span, from A.D. 950 to a similar termination date of A.D. 1200 (Dittert/Plog 80). Furthermore, in 1941, Colton by using an analysis of the paints, suggested that Snowflake Black-on-white was simply a variety of Reserve (Colton 41). This means that Snowflake Black-on-white would have been produced side by side with Reserve Black-on-white. This is very possible and further confused because Snowflake Black-on-white does not clearly follow the Cibola White Ware Style changes that we can observe in other types. For example,

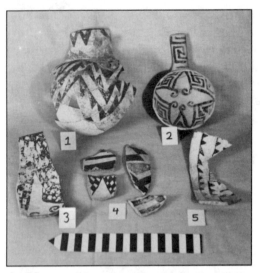

Photo 24. Snowflake Black-on-white ceramic examples. *This type exhibits solid motifs, less hachuring, and checkerboard patterns are common. A transition in style from the early Snowflake to late Snowflake can be observed with the Raven Site Ruins examples. The early Snowflakes resemble the northern Tusayan styles specifically "Sosi style" material, and the later ones begin to take on Tularosa characteristics.*

Reserve Black-on-white exhibits basically a Wingate Style, which evolves into a Tularosa Style very late in the type. One would expect Snowflake Black-on-white to exhibit design characteristics of the late Reserve material, i.e., Wingate Style, and later to show a shift to the Tularosa Style as the year A.D. 1200 approaches. This is true to some extent, but the problem is that Snowflake Black-on-white is, stylistically, copying the White Wares that were produced to the north, the Tusayan Styles. Tusayan Styles are not Cibola White Wares. They are a different animal. Snowflake Black-on-white copies a "Sosi Style" (which follows a northern Tusayan White Ware tradition). To further confuse the classification of Snowflake Black-on-white, the ceramic type has been used as a catchall category for any weird or unusual designs found in the Cibola White Ware distribution area.

I warned you that this would not be easy.

CONSTRUCTION — Vessels were made using the coil and scrape method. The paste is almost always either light or dark grey. Carbon streak is occasionally present. The temper is ground sherd, usually of medium grind. Inclusions are light grey and angular. The slip is usually a good white. Bowls are slipped on the interior and the exterior, jars on the exterior. Where the slip is very thick, it often flakes off and will exhibit crackling. The polish and overall execution of the finish on these vessels is good. Temper rarely protrudes through the slip.

The paint is mineral from the examples of Snowflake Black-on-white that have been excavated from Raven Site Ruins. William Longacre reports a Snowflake variety from Hay Hollow with an organic paint (Longacre 64). This mineral black at Raven Site Ruin is usually a good true black, fired in an oxygen-reducing atmosphere. Occasionally, this black paint will appear brown or reddish brown. These are probably the result of firing errors.

FORM — From the examples so far excavated from Raven Site Ruins, most of the vessels have been jars, not bowls. Small pitchers are common, as well as large ollas. There seems to be an increase in the creation of strange forms such as effigies.

The bowls that we have observed from the site are similar to those classified as Reserve Black-on-white. Sides are vertical, there is no incurve at the rim, and the lip is either the same thickness as the body of the bowl, or tapers to the lip. Lips of bowls are now often flattened.

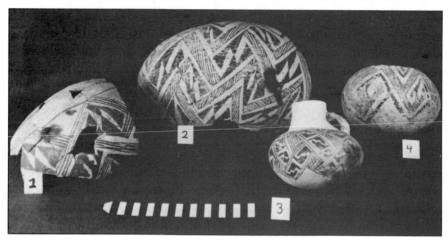

*Photo 24a. **Snowflake Black-on-white olla sections and jars.** Example 4 might be a late Reserve Black-on-white.*

PAINTED DESIGNS — Snowflake Black-on-white exhibits a predominance of solid units that are interlocked and little hachuring. Bowls often have an open bottom defined by a banding line. Wide interlocked terracing is common, as are checkerboards. The neck of jars often have wide parallel lines spaced quickly and evenly around the neck.

For the most part, Snowflake designs are copies of the northern Kayenta Styles that are not part of the Cibola White Ware tradition.

DISTRIBUTION — Snowflake Black-on-white shares a similar distribution as Reserve Black-on-white. This area centers in east/central Arizona, extending into western New Mexico, south to the Mogollon Rim and west to Snowflake, Arizona.

REMARKS — Snowflake Black-on-white is at least partially contemporaneous with Reserve Black-on-white and shares a similar distribution area. The later Snowflake ceramics from Raven Site

Ruins do appear to be evolving into the next Cibola White Ware in the sequence, i.e., Tularosa Black-on-white.

It is very difficult to distinguish Snowflake Black-on-white from the dozens of other black-on-white types that have been classified in the Southwest. This is particularly true if the provenance (origin) of the material is in question and/or you have only sherds to examine. Part of this problem is that Snowflake is a copy of the northern styles, even

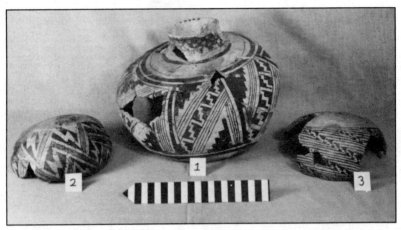

Photo 24b. Snowflake Black-on-white olla & jar bodies. *This ceramic type is difficult to differentiate from Tularosa Black-on-white, especially those vessels created later in the temporal range of the type.*

Photo 24c. Snowflake Black-on-white olla and bowl sections. *Checkerboard patterns are common. Example 5 shows a distinct Puerco style. The olla in Example 2 demonstrates the vertical lines on the neck of the olla which are a frequent treatment.*

though it is a Cibola White Ware and was produced to the south. All of this is further complicated by the fact that many ceramicists throw any material that they have trouble typing into the Snowflake Black-on-white pile.

TULAROSA BLACK-ON-WHITE

DATES — Tularosa Black-on-white was produced for about a one-hundred-year period, between A.D. 1200 and A.D.1300. Tularosa developes out of Reserve Black-on-white. The transition in painted design styles develops from a Wingate Style found on the reserve material to a later Tularosa Style found on Tularosa Black-on-white.

In the black-on-white ceramics and their temporal sequence, the temporal flow of style from one type to another seems to have been interrupted by Snowflake Black-on-white. Snowflake does not really fit very well into this developmental sequence, even though temporally it seems to fall into the right place. This is because Snowflake Black-on-white copies the northern ceramic styles. There are a few examples held in the White Mountain Archaeological Centers Collections where designs do seem to be developing toward the Tularosa Style.

Tularosa Black-on-white ceramics have been discovered in a tremendous abundance at Raven Site Ruins. This grand assemblage consists primarily of ollas. The greatest production period of this Tularosa material on the site seems to center near the later end of Tularosa's temporal line, i.e., A.D. 1280 to A.D. 1300. This Tularosa material is found in association primarily with St. Johns Polychrome ceramics.

Photo 25. Tularosa Black-on-white, olla glue-up sections. The raised areola around the neck of ollas is diagnostic to the type, as in Example 3. The star encircling the upper body of Examples 2 and 3 is also often seen. The interlocked spiral is the most common painted design.

Photo 25a. Tularosa Black-on-white jars. *Twisted handles are common as seen in Example 2, as are life forms used as handles. Example 4 uses a dog's head as a finger lug, and Example 5 (miniature) uses an eagle head.*

Photo 25b. Tularosa Black-on-white canteens and olla. *Example 1 is probably a late Snowflake Black-on-white. Examples 2 and 3 exhibit the raised areola which is diagnostic of the Tularosa ceramics.*

Photo 25c. Tularosa Black-on-white large glue-up sections. *Examples 1 and 2 demonstrate the raised areola, and in Example 3 the starburst around the upper body is seen. Example 4 is the only bowl of this type found, so far, at Raven Site Ruins.*

This indicates an expanded trading network at this time, and/or populational increases at the site. The prehistoric potters at Raven Site Ruins were producing these fine ceramics at an alarming rate, and trading them over a very wide area.

CONSTRUCTION — Vessels were made using the coil and scrape method. The paste is nearly always light to dark grey. A carbon streak is occasionally present. The temper is finely ground sherds. Any inclusions are light grey and angular.

The slip is a good white and well-polished. Tularosa vessels are the pinnacle of Cibola White Ware technology. They are beautifully executed, perfection seems to have been the goal of the Tularosa Black-on-white potters.

Photo 25d. Tularosa Black-on-white large ollas. Hachuring is much wider than the solid units. These jars are very globular. Notice the star bottom on Example 1, and the heavy fire clouds on Example 2.

Photo 25e. Tularosa Black-on-white dippers. Inter-locked terraced handle designs are common. Often there is a rattle in the handle, which makes noise when the dipper is in use.

The paint is a good black with a mineral base. This paint fires to a true black in a low oxygen atmosphere. Occasionally on one side of a large olla, this paint will appear brownish or red/brown. This indicates that on that side of the firing, a little air crept in. This turned the paint from good black to the brown or red/brown. This firing error is often observed on one small area of the olla only, but occasionally, the whole piece will be uniformly changed from a black-on-white to a brown, red/brown-on-white. Some of these firings with higher oxygen might have been an intentional attempt to create new colors.

FORM — The Tularosa Black-on-white material from Raven Site Ruins is very abundant. Out of all of this material, only one or two examples of bowls have been discovered. The predominant form of the Tularosa Black-on-white pottery is the olla, or large water jar. These are very round, almost a perfect circle. The neck of the jar goes straight up from the body, and the mouths of the ollas are small, even too small for the poor curator to put his/her hand into during restoration. Tularosa jars, ollas, and even canteens have unique features in form that are specific to this ceramic type. Recognizing these features is a key to recognizing Tularosa as a ceramic type.

Around the neck of Tularosa Black-on-white ollas, there often appears an areola. This is a raised area encircling the neck of the jar. These areolas are usually decorated in a contrasting design than the rest of the shoulder of the jar, which emphasizes their presence.

Photo 25f. Tularosa Black-on-white large ollas. Starburst design can be seen on Example 1 around the upper body. Notice the deliberate break in symmetry with the addition of the Pinedale style squiggles in one section of the star. Example 1 also exhibits the raised areola. Example 2 shows the simple star pattern at the bottom of the vessel.

Another form used in the creation of these vessels that is not unique to Tularosa Black-on-white, but is certainly a frequent occupance, is the use of effigy handles on small jars and mugs. These handles are commonly enhanced with life forms of dogs, mountain lions, birds and other animals. The few bowls that we have seen are thick, with in-curved rims, and a globular body.

There are several examples of small canteens, pitchers, dippers and mugs. These mugs and small jars often have twisted handles. The dippers have a variety of handles, including rounded (which is the most common), to square, cup-shaped, and even some with intentional rattles inside. The dippers with rattles in the handles were probably intended to make noise when the dipper was used. I doubt if this had any ceremonial significance, more likely the lady of the house wanted to hear when the dipper was being used, sort of an alarm on the refrigerator door.

One observation that I would like to record at this point in our examination of the ceramics from Raven Site Ruins, is the almost total absence of jars after the production of the Tularosa Black-on-white ceramics. The next jars in any quantity that we have observed at the site are the Matsaki Brown-on-buff varieties that were produced after A.D. 1400. We also see a large amount of re-utilized Tularosa ollas with many of the ceramic assemblages after A.D. 1300. Tularosa ollas are frequently found with other later ceramic assemblages, and these jars are very worn, foliated, and often repaired. It almost seems that jars were either not produced, or were produced in very limited numbers after A.D. 1300, i.e., after the Tularosa pottery, and were not again created in any large numbers until the introduction of the Matsaki material at A.D. 1400. For one hundred years they re-used the Tularosa ceramic jars instead of producing new ones. I can offer no explanation for this observation, except that perhaps, as excavations continue at Raven Site Ruins, the "missing link" in the jar assemblages will be discovered at some future date.

PAINTED DESIGNS — The painted designs on Tularosa Black-on-white pottery is applied to the exterior of jars, ollas, dippers, mugs and canteens; and the interior of bowls. The designs on Tularosa are tighter, there is less undecorated space, almost to the point of creating designs in the negative field. Solid units interlocked with identical hachured units with a white unpainted area between, are the norm. The hachuring usually is in parallel with the unit it fills. This hachuring is much finer than on the earlier Reserve Black-on-white ceramics.

The most distinctive element that you can learn to identify Tularosa Style and ceramics overall, is the use of the spiral. These spiral designs are interlocked; hachured, solid and negative with white space in between. A star design is often the defining border on the bottom of jars. This star design is also sometimes a part of the art work around the neck or shoulder of the jar. Interlocked terraced units often encompass the neck of the ollas and the handles on dippers.

DISTRIBUTION — Tularosa Black-on-white ceramic material is concentrated in the Upper Little Colorado River Drainage. It can be found to the east in New Mexico and as far west as Snowflake, Arizona, but these appearances are probably due to trade. Raven Site Ruins may well be the primary production center of Tularosa Black-on-white ceramics.

REMARKS — Tularosa Black-on-white is the finest Cibola White Ware from the Upper Little Colorado Drainage area. Vessels are perfectly formed and the art work is exceptional. For one hundred years the Raven Site Ruin potters produced this fine ceramic type and traded their work to other regions along with the polychrome ceramics that were contemporaneous.

Tularosa Black-on-white can usually be easily identified from other less recognizable Cibola White Wares. Vessel form is one key. The use of zoomorphic representations on handles and lugs, and the raised areola around the neck of ollas is diagnostic to the type. Painted designs include interlocked terraced units, interlocked hachured and solids with a white area between, and hachured units are tighter with finer line work than on previous Cibola White Wares. The use of the interlocked solid, hachured, and negative white spiral is a key painted design to quickly identify this beautiful ceramic type.

PINEDALE BLACK-ON-WHITE

Pinedale Black-on-white ceramics were produced at the same time as Pinedale Black-on-red and Pinedale Polychrome i.e., A.D. 1275 to A.D. 1325. This ceramic type overlaps with the later Tularosa Black-on-white ceramics. Pinedale Black-on-white could well be the very last black-on-white type that was produced at Raven Site Ruins.

By A.D. 1300, a lot was happening at Raven Site Ruins with ceramic technology. The "new" glaze paints were becoming popular, and later in the 1300s new slip applications were being tried. Black-on-white pottery basically disappeared sometime shortly after A.D. 1300 at Raven Site Ruins, and it was probably phased out in favor of the polychrome ceramics.

CONSTRUCTION — Vessels were formed using the coil and scrape method. Pinedale Black-on-white shares all of the features common to the other Cibola White Wares, including grey paste, sherd temper, good white slip and true black mineral paint.

FORM — No Pinedale Black-on-white bowls have been discovered at Raven Site Ruins. One large olla and two dippers make up the entire ceramic assemblage of this ceramic type from the ruin. It is very difficult to distinguish Pinedale Black-on-white from other Cibola White Wares if only sherds are available for analysis.

The vessel forms are similar to those forms found on Tularosa Black-on-white material. The dippers have slightly thicker body walls and the olla has a smaller neck and mouth. The body of the olla is more globular.

PAINTED DESIGNS — Pinedale Black-on-white ceramics follow the Pinedale Style (see Ceramic Styles). There is basically more use of solid units and hachuring is confined to simple parallel lines in bordered zones. Banding lines define areas of the design elements, creating specific fields for the designs.

The olla shown in Photo 26 demonstrates this restricted use of space. The neck of the olla has simple lines around the neck. You might compare this line work treatment on the neck of ollas to Snowflake Black-on-white, which often exhibits lines that are vertical. The shoulder of the olla is free of designs. The design field on the body of the olla is confined to a narrow zone, which is also defined by banding lines.

Photo 26. Pinedale Black-on-white olla and dippers. *This ceramic type is probably the last black-on-white ceramics that were produced at Raven Site Ruins. Shortly after A.D.1300, the black-on-white ceramics were phased out in favor of the polychromes.*

DISTRIBUTION — Pinedale Black-on-white has the same distribution area as Pinedale Polychrome and Pinedale Black-on-red. These types can be found in the Zuni area on the north/east, west to the Verde River, south to the Sonoran border and as far south as Casas Grandes. The core area of production is west of the Little Colorado River, from Roosevelt Lake to Cherry Creek.

REMARKS — Pinedale Black-on-white is probably the last black-on-white ceramic type that was produced at Raven Site Ruins. There is some question as to whether or not the Pinedale ceramics were produced at the site, or traded in, being that the core areas of production are further west. However, the Pinedale ceramics fit well into the ceramic sequence which developed at Raven Site Ruins, and they were undoubtedly produced at the ruins.

SOCORRO BLACK-ON-WHITE

DATES — This ceramic type was produced from A.D. 950 until A.D. 1400. Only one example has been found at Raven Site Ruins. This large olla top was excavated from the north pueblo area, and was found with ceramic assemblages that would suggest that it dates between A.D. 1000 and A.D. 1100.

CONSTRUCTION — Vessels were formed using the coil and scrape method. The paste is light grey, with dark grey to black angular inclusions. The temper is ground sherds. The slip is a good white, well polished and finished. The paint is mineral, and a good black.

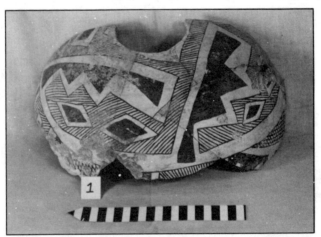

Photo 27. Socorro Black-on-white olla top. This ceramic type was produced for many centuries from A.D. 950 to A.D. 1400. This vessel may have been traded to Raven Site Ruins from the east. Very little of this type has been discovered at the site. This vessel does display the characteristics of the Raven Site Cibola White Wares, such as clay body, temper and mineral paint.

FORM — Socorro Black-on-white ollas are usually large, with globular bodies. The mouths are small and the necks are vertical. The shoulder area of the ollas are rounded and large. The example shown in Photo 27 from Raven Site Ruins shows how the neck of the olla has been completely worn away from use. Flat stone lids were often employed to cover these ollas. Placing the stone lid on the mouth of the olla slowly wore the neck away. This wear demonstrates that this olla was used a very long time.

PAINTED DESIGNS — The painted designs on Socorro Black-on-white are easy to distinguish. Large clean fields of hachured units combined with solid units with a white area in between predominate. We have observed very similar design layouts on several of the Cibola White Wares, however, Socorro Black-on-white can be recognized by the large scale of the designs which often lack symmetry. There are usually large undecorated areas, and the overall layout appears eclectic.

DISTRIBUTION — Socorro Black-on-white is believed to have spread into the Rio Grande area from the west. It is usually found south of Albuquerque, New Mexico to Socorro, New Mexico.

REMARKS — Socorro Black-on-white was produced for a long time prehistorically. The type has been split into several variations based on design changes over this long temporal depth. The two recognized variations are Chupadero Black-on-white and Casa Colorado Black-on-white. Both are found south and south/east of the core area for Socorro Black-on-white.

Chapter 7

Trade Wares at Raven Site Ruins

Most of the vessels that were traded to Raven Site Ruins came from the south, below the Mogollon Rim. There are very few ceramic examples that arrived from north of the site. There is an abundance of painted ceramics found at the site in the south pueblo areas that were not made at Raven Site Ruins. These are very easy to recognize because of the differences in temper, pigments and overall execution, from the indigenous Raven Site Ruins ceramic material. There are at least five different trade wares from the south, these are the Salado Polychromes including Pinto Polychrome, Pinto Black-on-red, Gila Polychrome, Tonto Polychrome, and Salado Red.

One example of Tonto Polychrome has been found at Raven Site Ruins that was produced at the site. This prehistoric copy is of better quality than the original Tonto Polychrome examples that were traded in.

PINTO POLYCHROME

DATES — There is considerable debate concerning the dates of the Salado Polychromes. Pinto Polychrome was produced between A.D.1150 and A.D. 1250 according to the early work of Harold Colton and Lyndon Hargrave (Colton/Hargrave 37). Carlson suggests that Pinto Polychrome was produced between A.D. 1275 and as late as A.D. 1400 and he considers this type to be related in design to Pinedale Polychrome and Fourmile Polychrome (Carlson 82). Several examples of this type

Photo 28. Pinto Polychrome Bowls. *The interior center is left unpainted. Example 2 has large areas of the white slip that has flaked off because this slip is not polished after it is applied.*

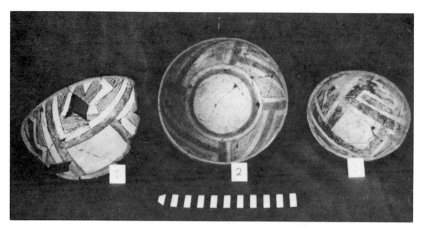

Photo 28a. Pinto Polychrome Bowls. The hachured and solid units are often nearly the same size. Occasionally the solid units are even slightly larger than those that are hachured.

have been discovered at Raven Site Ruins. These were traded in from below the Mogollon Rim. They were not made at Raven Site Ruins.

CONSTRUCTION — These vessels were made using the coil and scrape method. They were fired in an oxidizing atmosphere. The body of the clay is usually brick red, or tan, and rarely grey to black. Carbon streaks are common. The temper is sand, usually water-worn.

Bowls are slipped lightly with red on the exteriors and with a thick creamy white on the interiors. The interiors are well-smoothed but they are not polished. This interior white slip is usually thickly applied and it often flakes off the surface of the vessel in large areas. This slip

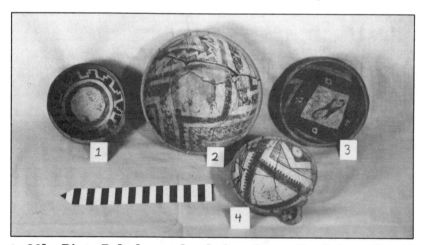

Photo 28b. Pinto Polychrome bowls from Raven Site Ruins. Wide black bands define the undecorated center of the bowl. These bands are then incorporated into the designs on the walls of the bowl.

does not survive preservation well, undoubtedly because it was not polished into the surface of the vessel. The exterior red slip is lightly polished. Bowl interiors are painted with a black paint on the white slip. The paint is carbon-based and it ranges from thick and densely applied to thin and watery.

FORM — Only bowls have been found so far at Raven Site Ruins. There is quite a diversity in the sizes that have been found. Small bowls no larger than 4.5 inches in diameter are common from Raven Site Ruins, and ranging up to over 14 inches in diameter. This is a much greater diversity of sizes than we have observed with any other ceramic type so far discovered. Rims are simple, often with a slight bevel toward the interior of the bowl. Occasionally there is a slight thickening of the rim. Smaller bowls are usually deeper than larger examples. Pinto Polychrome bowls exhibit far less diversity in rim treatment than many of the White Mountain Red Ware ceramic types.

Photo 28c. Pinto Polychrome bowls from Raven Site Ruins.

Photo 28d. Pinto Polychrome bowls with center bottom designs.

PAINTED DESIGNS — Bowl interiors are decorated, exteriors are not. Usually, the bottom interior of the bowl is left unpainted, leaving a circle, square or triangular area. Designs usually carry to the rim without upper banding lines. The unpainted area at the bottom of the bowl is usually banded by wide lines that are incorporated into the designs around the interior walls of the bowl. Swastikas in quartered layouts are common. Designs are usually hachured and solid units with white areas between. The hatchuring and solid elements are nearly the same width, although hachured units are often slightly larger.

DISTRIBUTION — Pinto Polychrome is found primarily south of Raven Site Ruins below the Mogollon Rim in the Roosevelt Basin, east of Roosevelt Dam.

REMARKS — Pinto Polychrome demonstrates an early use of an overall white slip on the interior of bowls. The unpainted area at the center bottom of the bowl later becomes covered with designs with the next stage of ceramic development in this ceramic series as is seen on Gila Polychromes. Several examples of Pinto Polychromes exhibit designs that cover the entire interior of the vessel, these are probably transitional to the Gila Polychromes.

PINTO BLACK-ON-RED

DATES — Pinto Black-on-red is contemporaneous with Pinto Polychrome dating between A.D. 1275 and A.D. 1400.

REMARKS — Construction, form, painted design and distribution of Pinto Black-on-red vessels are identical to Pinto Polychrome except

Photo 29. Pinto Black-on-red bowls. *These are identical to Pinto Polychromes except that no white slip was used.*

that there is no white slip used on this ceramic type. Bowls are covered with an overall thin red slip, interior and exterior, and designs are painted on the interior of bowls using a thin black carbon-based paint.

Pinto Black-on-red vessels were traded to Raven Site Ruins along with the Pinto Polychromes. The sand temper used to construct both of these trade wares helps identify them from the ceramics that were produced at Raven Site Ruins.

GILA POLYCHROME

DATES — The dates for Gila Polychrome are often debated. This ceramic type was produced around A.D. 1300 (Colton/Hargrave 37). Other researchers have concluded that this ceramic type was produced between A.D. 1250 and as late as A.D. 1400 (Dittert/Plog 80) and A.D. 1300 to perhaps as late as A.D. 1600 (Cordell 84).

CONSTRUCTION — Vessels were produced using the coil and scrape method and were fired in an oxidizing atmosphere. The body of the clay is brick red to tan, and sometimes grey. The clay temper is water-worn sand. Bowl interiors are thickly slipped white to cream, and the slip is not polished. Bowl exteriors are thinly slipped in red and well-polished.

Bowl interiors are painted with black on the white slip. The pigment is carbon-based, black, dense and thickly applied.

FORM — Only bowls have been found at Raven Site Ruins. These are deep with flaring rims. The rims are beveled or lipped outward. There is no thickening at the rim. These flaring rims are incorporated into the painted designs using sets of wavy lines encircling the interior rim of the bowl.

PAINTED DESIGNS — The exterior is left unpainted. Bowls interiors are decorated with an overall layout. There is usually no unpainted area at the center bottom as we have observed with Pinto Polychrome and Pinto Black-on-red. The decoration never carries to the rim. The rim area receives a very special treatment. The rim flare formed in the clay, is often painted with a set of parallel wavy lines near the top of the rim, followed by a solid black band which encircles the rim but is broken once. Gila Polychromes usually exhibit this use of the spirit break (see *The Ceramic Spirit Break*, page 148). Solid designs are most common, accompanied by areas with simple parallel lines. Ticking and spirals are common as is simple hatchuring that fills triangular zones.

DISTRIBUTION — Gila Polychromes were produced south of the Mogollon Rim and traded to Raven Site Ruins. Gila Polychromes are found primarily in the Roosevelt Basin and Tonto Basin. This type was widely traded, and sherds have been found as far as the Verde Valley,

San Pedro Valley, Globe, Safford, Winslow, Ajo, Gila Bend, and Nogales, Arizona. This type occasionally is found east and south to El Paso, Texas and Casas Grandes, Mexico.

REMARKS — Gila Polychrome was widely traded throughout the Southwest. It is contemporaneous with several other ceramics that use the overall white interior slips. The role of this ceramic type in the development of the later pueblo ceramics is still hotly debated. Many researchers believe that Gila Polychromes were produced even later than A.D. 1400.

Photo 30. Gila Polychrome bowls. *This ceramic type was widely traded and produced late in prehistory. Use of the spirit break is common on this ceramic type. Distinct form changes flaring the rim of the bowls and incorporating a zone of design within the flare is a frequent treatment.*

TONTO POLYCHROME

DATES — The dates for Tonto Polychrome range in the literature from A.D. 1300 to A.D. 1400+. Most researchers feel that this ceramic type developed out of the Pinto and Gila Polychrome sequence but arrived slightly later than Gila Polychrome, dating the type beginning at about A.D. 1350 and continuing possibly as late as A.D. 1600 (Cordell 84). At Raven Site Ruins, Tonto Polychromes are found in association with ceramics that date after A.D. 1400.

CONSTRUCTION — Vessels were made using the coil and scrape method, and were fired in an oxidizing atmosphere. The body of the clay ranges from brick red to tan and sometimes grey. One example from Raven Site Ruins exhibits a black core resulting from the use of scoria as a temper. This example was produced at Raven Site Ruins, and was not traded in, as were the other examples discovered at the site. Carbon streaks are common. The temper is fine water-worn sand.

Only Tonto Polychrome jars have so far been discovered at Raven Site Ruins. Jars are coated with white and red slip in different areas of design. These slips are well-polished. The black paint is carbon-based and dense. It is very thickly applied.

FORM — The Tonto Polychrome jars from Raven Site Ruins are large, wide-mouthed and have squat bodies. The shoulder areas bulge and then quickly taper to the bottom. Jar rims flare outward with an outward lip.

PAINTED DESIGNS — Red slipped areas predominate the exterior of jars. Areas of white slip are applied in conjunction with the red and then black designs are painted on the white slipped areas. The black designs leave a small edge of white around the black as an outline. Hatchuring is rare, and the design field is concentrated on the shoulder and neck of the olla, never extending too far toward the bottom of the vessel. The neck of the olla is treated as a specific design field. The wavy parallel lines common to Gila Polychromes are often present on the neck. Brush work is free, bold and rather careless.

DISTRIBUTION — Tonto Polychrome ceramics are concentrated below the Mogollon Rim in the Roosevelt Basin in the area of Globe, Arizona. Several examples have been found at Raven Site Ruins, including one vessel that was produced at the site and not traded in.

REMARKS — Tonto Polychrome ceramics probably evolved out of the

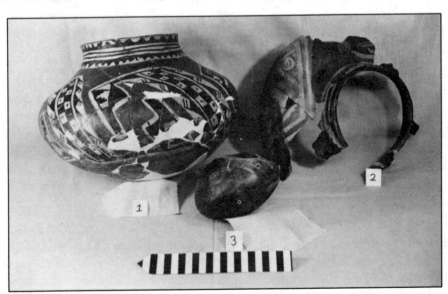

Photo 31. Tonto Polychrome ollas from Raven Site Ruins. These examples have a fine sand temper and they were traded to the site from the south, below the Mogollon Rim.

Pinto and Gila Polychromes. They may have been produced very late in prehistory, some researchers extend their production well beyond A.D. 1400. At Raven Site Ruins all of the Tonto Polychrome examples so far discovered have been found in association with other ceramic assemblages that post-date A.D. 1400.

Photo 31a. Tonto Polychrome olla. *This example was produced at Raven Site Ruins. It has a scoria temper, it is high-fired and very thickly slipped. This prehistoric copy is of a better quality than the Tonto Polychrome originals. Tonto Polychromes were normally produced south of Raven Site Ruins, below the Mogollon Rim.*

Chapter 8

The Corrugated Ceramics
of Raven Site Ruins

Corrugated ceramics were primarily utilized for cooking. The indented or incised surface creates a greater surface area for the transfer of heat from the cooking fire to the contents of the vessel. Other theories that have been presented attribute the presence of the corrugations to

Photo 32. Reserve Indented Corrugated jars. *Variations in the patterning of the corrugations are usually reflected in the type name. These vessels were used for cooking and for storage.*

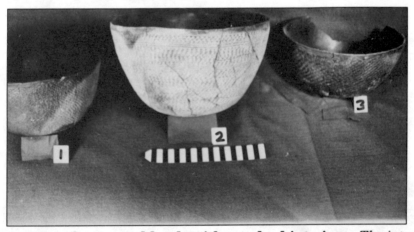

Photo 32a. Corrugated bowls with smudged interiors. *The interior smudging often has a gunmetal iridescence. Example 2 is probably a Tularosa Patterned Corrugated.*

keeping the vessel from slipping during the frequent handling, or to lessen the possibility of the vessel breaking from the thermal shock of putting it repeatedly back into the fire.

Assigning a date to corrugated ceramics is a little like trying to assign a date to an old cast-iron skillet. These vessels were made for a very long period of time and they changed very little over the centuries. There has been little research to contribute to the dating of these ceramics, with the exception of a few distinctive types.

Photo 32b. Linear Banded Corrugated bowls *with smudged interiors.*

Photo 32c. Corrugated jars and olla bottom. *Example 2 is the bottom of a very large jar that was broken and then re-used, possibly as a cover or smoker. The hole in the bottom was deliberately punched out.*

Photo 32d. Tularosa Fillet Rim bowls with smudged interiors. These rather distinctive bowls were produced between A.D. 1100 and A.D. 1250.

Photo 32e. Salado Red Corrugated bowls. Several of these examples have smudged interiors. They are found in association with the Pinto, Gila, and Tonto Polychrome ceramic assemblages.

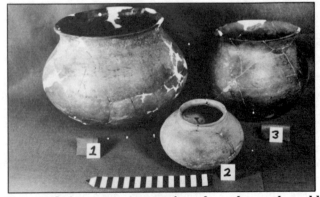

Photo 32f. Large plain ware storage jars from the south pueblo at Raven Site Ruins. Example 1 has a smudged interior. These large ollas with very wide mouths are found in the south pueblo area of Raven Site Ruins and they were produced after A.D. 1400.

Chapter 9

Styles of the White Mountain Red Wares & Cibola White Wares

Throughout our discussion of the White Mountain Red Wares and the Cibola White Wares there has been repeated reference to different ceramic styles. In ceramic analysis, the style refers to the similarities that can be observed in the overall layout of patterns, motifs, fields of design, framing, banding and hachuring. If the observation is made that a specific ceramic type exhibits, for example, Tularosa "style", this means that the vessel shares patterns and designs that are lumped together into what researchers recognize as frequently found on Tularosa ceramics. Remember, style transcends type. Style is the genus, type is the species. There may be several ceramic types that share the same style. By recognizing the style of a prehistoric vessel, it is possible in a gross way, to recognize the temporal span when that style was used, and even if the vessel type is questionable, a calendar date can be assigned.

One of the confusions that I have observed on the faces of bewildered students during discussions of style and type, is the fact that most of the ceramic styles are named after a specific ceramic type, even though the style can be found on several other ceramic types. Tularosa Black-on-white is a specific ceramic type. It exhibits, most clearly and most frequently, the designs and patterns that are called Tularosa Style. Tularosa Style can be found on not only Tularosa Black-on-white, but also on Wingate Black-on-red, Wingate Polychrome, St. Johns Black-on-red, St. Johns Polychrome and occasionally on other White Mountain types.

The following material is relevant only to the White Mountain Red Wares and the Cibola White Wares. The Zuni Glaze Wares will not be analyzed in regard to style, primarily because they begin with the very distinctive Heshotauthla ceramics and then rapidly deteriorate in design execution with the use of the glaze paint. Heshotauthla does have a distinctive "style" or group of painted characteristics unique to the type, but as the use of additional white slip increases, the painted patterns of the later ceramics in the series are not as important as the colors and color combinations that were achieved.

HOLBROOK STYLE

Holbrook Style can be seen on ceramics that date between A.D. 1000 and around A.D. 1150. In the White Mountain Red Ware series, Holbrook Style can be seen only on the Puerco Black-on-red ceramics. It also can be found on several other black-on-white ceramics including Holbrook Black-on-white, Puerco Black-on-white and on Escavada Black-on-white.

Holbrook Style ceramics have *only* solid motifs. There is never any hachuring. Common patterns are interlocked frets, sometimes with the inclusion of barbs on the ends. Sometimes dots are attached to the frets. Patterns are symmetrical. The layout is banded, and on bowl interiors the design is restricted to the walls of the bowl.

Figure 12. Holbrook Style. *Holbrook Style exhibits solid motifs only, there is never any hachuring present. (From Carlson 70)*

PUERCO STYLE

Puerco Style can be found on a variety of ceramic types that date between A.D. 1000 and A.D. 1200. In the White Mountain Red Ware series, it can be found on Puerco Black-on-red, and only rarely on Wingate Polychrome, St. Johns Black-on-red, St. Johns Polychrome, and Pinedale Polychrome. It is the most commonly found of Puerco Black-on-white ceramics.

Puerco Style is distinct in that it exhibits solid and hachured motifs that do not interlock with each other. Solid motifs and checkerboard patterns are also common. The hachuring is wide-lined and usually parallel. The hachured or checkerboard units alternate with the solid units. Solid units are frets or rectangles, often negative rectangles are created. Pendants with barbs and dot appendages occur. On bowl interiors, the designs are restricted to the walls of the bowl.

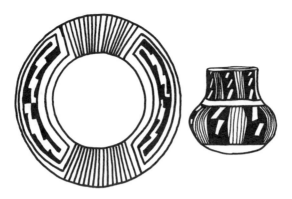

Figure 13. Puerco Style. Hachuring appears combined with solid units, but the two are never interlocked. The hachuring is usually parallel and wide. Sometimes checkerboards are used instead of hachures. (From Carlson 70)

WINGATE STYLE

Wingate Style can be found on ceramics that were produced between A.D. 1000 and A.D. 1200. It is commonly found on Wingate Black-on-red and on the earlier versions of Wingate Polychrome. Occasional examples are seen on St. Johns Polychrome. Wingate Style is common on Reserve Black-on-white ceramics and Gallup Black-on-white.

The important thing to notice about Wingate Style is the use of interlocked hachured and solid units and the hachuring is *always* wider than the solid units. Both diagonal and parallel hachuring is common. The designs on bowl interiors usually focus on the walls of the bowl, but occasionally the entire interior will be covered with designs. Patterns are symmetrical, the execution is very good and the lines that frame the hachured areas are the same width as the hachuring.

Figure 14. Wingate Style. The hachured and solid units are interlocked and the hachured units are always larger than the solid units. (From Carlson 70)

TULAROSA STYLE

Vessels that exhibit the Tularosa Style were made between A.D. 1200 and A.D. 1300. There are many ceramic types that exhibit the Tularosa Style. This is because there was a blossoming of new ceramic creativity around A.D. 1300 and Tularosa Style was the standard format at the time. Tularosa Style can be found on the later examples of Wingate Polychrome, and on St. Johns Black-on-red, St. Johns Polychrome, and Springerville Polychrome. It is occasionally seen on Pinedale Polychrome, Pinedale Black-on-red, Kwakina Polychrome and Heshotauthla Polychrome. The most frequent appearance of the Tularosa Style is on the Tularosa Black-on-white ceramics that are found in such abundance at Raven Site Ruins.

Solid units are interlocked with hachured units. The hachured units are large with complex edges and the solid units are medium and they basically follow the same form as the hachured units. These patterns are very tight, the vessels will often look crowded. The hachuring can be parallel to the unit it fills, or diagonal, or even mixed. The hachured areas (as compared to the solid areas) are smaller than those seen in the Wingate Style, but they are still slightly larger than the solid units. An unpainted area of white slip often outlines the solid black motifs. One distinctive motif found in the Tularosa Style is the interlocked, hachured and solid, spiral. This treatment of the spiral does occasionally occur in the Wingate Style, but it is very frequently observed in the Tularosa Style.

Figure 15. Tularosa Style. The hachured areas are now smaller than those seen with the Wingate Style, but they are still slightly larger than the solid motifs. The interlocked hachured and solid spiral is a very common motif. (From Carlson 70)

PINEDALE STYLE

Pinedale Style appears around A.D. 1300 and remains popular late into the 1300s. Pinedale Style is transitional from the standard Tularosa Style to the new and radically different Fourmile Style late in the 14th century. It plays a major role in the development of many of the new ceramic types that were created after A.D. 1300 (see *Development of the Katsina Cult,* page 135). The development of the Pinedale Style and then later the Fourmile Style reflect other social changes that were occurring at the same time, including the development of the Katsina Cult in the White Mountains of Arizona.

Pinedale Style can be found on Pinedale Black-on-red, Pinedale Polychrome, Cedar Creek Polychrome, and less frequently on very late examples of St. Johns Polychrome. There are a lot of examples in the White Mountain Archaeological Centers Collections from Raven Site Ruins where a vessel will appear to be a bastard combination of St. Johns Polychrome, Heshotauthla Polychrome, with a Pinedale Style twist. Many of the Heshotauthla vessels clearly have a Pinedale Style influence, especially the squiggle patterns in black over a white slip. If ceramicists can learn to recognize all of the influences exhibited on a single vessel, then assigning a date to that particular ceramic piece is not only more accurate, but more relevant to custom, culture and cultural change.

Pinedale Style often focuses on the entire vessel, as if the form of the vessel creates the field of design, and not vice versa. Bowl interiors

Figure 16. Pinedale Style. *Transitional from Tularosa Style to Fourmile Style. Clean, crisp patterns and execution usher in the new era of asymmetry. (From Carlson 70)*

utilize not just the interior walls but often the entire slipped interior. However, there is not a focus on the center of the bowl. This comes later, with the progression to the Fourmile Style. We still see interlocked and hachured units, but the solid units are larger and they stand out from the field of design. Patterns are cleaner, crisp, less busy than the Tularosa Style. There is an increase in the use of "squiggles" in black over-lain on white and red. Remember in Tularosa Style when we noted that the interlock spiral was diagnostic? With the Pinedale Style, the squiggle, executed in black, on a white or red background, opposing the area of design is a diagnostic flag to the recognition of this ceramic style, but not; unfortunately, to the ceramic type "Pinedale".

There is a throwback to earlier styles in that banding, or creating an isolated field of design, again becomes important. This also includes double banding.

Life forms appear, often birds, but they are very geometric, usually created by adding the curved beak and tail feathers to a simple triangle. This is very common in the later Zuni Glaze Wares. Patterns are symmetrical. The art work and overall execution is excellent.

FOURMILE STYLE

Fourmile Style appears just after A.D. 1300 and survives as a major influence in the White Mountains of Arizona until around A.D. 1400. Even after A.D. 1400, copies in ceramics of this style survive well into the 15th century, as Point of Pines Polychromes. Fourmile ceramics reflect a shift in social custom, from traditional-controlled-space-order, to radical-free-creative-disorder. Something was shaking up the system. These dramatic changes in ceramics during this temporal period have not gone unnoticed. The development of the Katsina Cult in the White Mountains of Arizona is believed to have occurred at the same time. The appearance of square and rectangular kivas and kiva murals share the same dates. Links between these stylistic ceramic changes and prehistoric social customs are hotly debated.

Fourmile Style can be observed on only an elite few ceramic types sharing a brief temporal span, i.e., Fourmile Polychrome, Showlow Polychrome and Kinishba Polychrome (Carlson 70). It also appears on Point of Pines Polychrome, however, this ceramic type is a poor copy of the original, dating well after A.D. 1400 and should not be included while discussing stylistic changes.

On bowl interiors, the field of design not only encompasses the entire surface, it dominates. The center bottom of the interior bowl is now the focus, the walls of the bowl are secondary but utilized to contain the design in a way that frames but does not control.

Motifs are bold and asymmetrical. There is no interlocking of any unit with any other. Hachuring still occurs, but only to enhance specific motifs. The hachuring is perfectly executed, and usually parallel to the motif. Zoomorphs are created out of spirals and triangles. It seems that previously geometric figures grow tail feathers and become birds.

All motifs have wide framing lines, even those that are hachured have framing lines that are wider than the hachuring itself. Black motifs are edged in thin white kaolin.

Wide black banding edged in white encircles most vessels on the interior and exterior. Spirit breaks are common (see *Ceramic Spirit Break,* page 148). The Fourmile Style potters began to create images on ceramics that contain meaningful symbolism (see *Symbols,* page 139).

Figure 17. Fourmile Style. *The Fourmile Style is unique to very few ceramic types, and it survived only briefly in prehistory. The stylistic changes that occurred between A.D. 1325 and A.D. 1400 reflect the larger social and cultural shifts of the late 14th century. (From Carlson 70)*

Chapter 10

Miniatures & Clay Fetishes

MINIATURE CERAMIC VESSELS

One of the joys of excavating a prehistoric site that is as culturally rich as Raven Site Ruins, is the frequent discovery of miniature vessels. These often survive intact because of their small size. However, debate often arises as to their function. The most frequent conclusion is that they were made for children as toys. Some are so crudely formed that they were undoubtedly created by the children themselves. To dismiss all of the miniatures as toys is probably erroneous. If you examine the containers that are necessary for day-to-day activities anywhere in the world, you will quickly discover the need for very small vessels. These could have contained paint, medicines, pollen, or anything else that was used in small/precious quantities.

The small dippers that are shown in Photo 33, Examples 1 and 2, are probably the equivalent of a kitchen soup spoon with a pragmatic function in the preparation of food. The very crude jars, Examples 9, 10, 12, 14 and 16 appear to have been produced by inexperienced hands, possibly children. In fact, Example 12, clearly exhibits the finger imprints of very small hands. Example 11 is of particular interest in that it is a specific ceramic type. This is a miniature Tularosa Black-on-white jar, dating between A.D. 1200 and A.D. 1300 and exhibits an effigy finger lug.

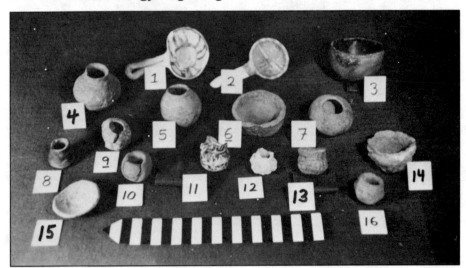

Photo 33. Miniature ceramic vessels. *These are usually dismissed as toys even though several examples may have had a pragmatic function.*

CLAY FETISHES

Some objects that are made out of ceramic that are discovered at the site are not vessels or containers. The most frequent non-vessel that is made from fired clay are the prehistoric fetishes representing animals of various species.

According to legend, each animal represents a directional significance associated with a color. North is the mountain lion, west is the bear, south is the badger, the east is the wolf, above is the eagle and below is the mole. The associated colors are: yellow to the north, blue to the west, red to the south, white to the east, all colors above and black below (Cushing 1883). Even though each animal has a specific color and directional significance, each animal also has a "younger brother". For example, the mountain lion is given the directional and color representation of north and yellow, but he has younger brothers in the west that are represented by mountain lion forms that are blue, in the east that are white, in the south that are red, above that are spotted and below that are black. This means that you could find a fetish that represents a wolf, eagle, mole, mountain lion, bear or badger with any of the color representations. These fetishes were used by the prehistoric hunters to insure the success of the hunt. They were carried in a small crescent-shaped bag of buckskin and hung over the hunter's heart by a buckskin thong.

Fetishes can be made from clay, carved from minerals that are of the correct color for each specific representation, or created from a naturally occurring stone with similarities to the animal's shape. These naturally occurring fetishes are highly prized because of the belief that they are what is left of the original animals of the earth, before the earth was "hardened".

According to legend, Sun Father created two children, and gave them a bow (rainbow) and arrows (lightning). The earth was covered with water, and in order for man to survive on the surface, the children of Father Sun saw that it was necessary to harden and dry the surface. They performed a ceremony using a shield (also supplied by Sun Father) and the rainbow and the lightning. Fire rolled over the face of the earth and the earth was hardened. The children of Sun Father also hardened and burnt the original animals of the earth so that they would not devour humankind (Cushing 1881). The naturally occurring concretions and rock forms that have similarities to animals are believed to be the original animals of the earth that were burnt and hardened. These were prized more highly for use as fetishes than fetishes that are carved or created from clay.

Photo 34 exhibits thirteen different fetishes that have been discovered at Raven Site Ruins. Examples 1, 2, 3, 5, 6, 7, are formed from clay and lightly fired. Examples 9, 12, and 13 are naturally occurring stone specimens that vaguely resemble different animals. Example 4 probably represents a dog or wolf. This specimen is wonderfully preserved. Even the sinew cord and attached beads and point are intact. Example 8 is a slightly modified antelope bone. This use of this particular bone as a fetish is fairly common, due to its natural shape which resembles a quadruped. Examples 10 and 11 are eagles, which are very stylized. Carvings representing the wings and tail feathers can be seen. These two pieces may not be fetishes, but simply ornaments. Example 10 is carved from a limestone mineral that is white to buff, and Example 11 is carved from a copper-based mineral similar to turquoise which is blue/green.

Among the ceramic fetishes shown in Photo 34, Example 6 is a parrot. Very often from Raven Site Ruins birds made from clay are used as lugs on canteens and small jars. This is particularly common with the Tularosa ceramic assemblages dating between A.D. 1200 and A.D. 1300. Example 1 is probably a bear and Example 3 could be a weasel. It is often very difficult to determine what animal is being represented. For example, several of these fetishes appear to be dogs, including Examples 2, 4, 5, and 7. However, according to Zuni legend, the wolf (dog) is supposed to be represented with the tail down, not up. All of the examples that we have discovered from Raven Site Ruins that look like dogs/wolves/coyotes have the tail up. It is very possible, that the legends and use of fetishes recorded by Cushing in the late 19th century have only a slight similarity to the uses and legends surrounding fetishes that were used prehistorically.

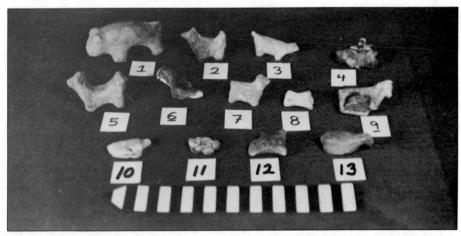

Photo 34. *Fetishes from Raven Site Ruins made from clay, mineral, bone, and naturally-shaped stone.*

Chapter 11

The Prehistoric Re-use
of Broken Ceramic Vessels

As the archaeologist excavates, he/she is very careful to recover all of the information possible. Every flake of flint, every fractured bone, and every sherd of ceramic is painstakingly recorded, lightly cleaned, and catalogued.

After all of the analysis is complete, the curators in the lab will attempt to re-assemble the broken sherds of ceramic into complete vessels. From a single room at Raven Site Ruins that measures only three meters by three meters, with a depth to floor of only a meter and a half, it is not uncommon to recover tens of thousands of sherds. This abundance of ceramic material is usually found in the trash middens. Attempting to re-assemble these broken pieces into whole vessels is like taking a thousand jigsaw puzzles, mixing them together, throwing a few handfuls of pieces away, burying them for a thousand years, digging them up, cleaning them off, and then attempting to piece the puzzles together, without pictures to go by. Remember, these are not only three dimensional puzzles, but actually fourth dimensional, factoring in the different temporal periods in which they were produced.

The sherds are typed and counted during the ceramic analysis. This begins the sorting process. Corrugated material is separated from black-on-white material, black-on-red from polychrome. This process alone may continue for several weeks.

The glue-up begins by using a reversible bonding agent and joining any piece that correctly matches any other. After several months of joining pieces, vessels seem to grow out of the surface of the lab tables a sherd at a time. You may have noticed throughout the text, examples of large glue-up sections. These are often very poorly reconstructed, with pieces stuck haphazardly on the surface. The reconstruction of these pieces is by no means complete. At Raven Site Ruins vessels emerge a sherd at a time from over very large areas of the site. It may take several years to find enough sherds of a single vessel to attempt a more complete reconstruction. Usually, when over 85% to 95% of a vessel has been found, it is then disassembled using a solvent to dissolve the glue, and then reassembled into its original form.

However, most often, all of the missing pieces of the vessel are not present in the ceramic assemblage from the excavation. *Where did they go? Could they have been missed by the excavators?* All of the earth that is removed during excavations at Raven Site Ruins is screened through one-eighth inch mesh, not once, but twice. If the missing pieces of the vessels are not amongst the sherds from the room, or provenance of the excavation, then they simply were not there to begin with.

There are several explanations that could account for the absence of all of the pieces of a ceramic vessel from a single room. Many of these rooms were multiple stories high. If a vessel was originally located on the roof of the room, or on an upper floor, it could have broken and scattered into areas that encompass more than just the area of a single room. We have observed this many times during the excavations at Raven Site Ruins. Part of a vessel will be discovered in a room, and the rest of the same vessel will be found several years later as excavations continue in neighboring rooms. If this were the only reason that pieces were missing from the vessels, then theoretically, all of the pieces could be discovered as excavations continue.

If the ceramic assemblage is from a trash midden, it is far more likely that most of the vessels will be incompletely represented. Imagine, a vessel is accidentally broken prehistorically and the pieces are thrown into the trash. All of the pieces probably would not be perfectly manuported to the same trash midden. Some would undoubtedly be lost along the way.

The above discussion does not really address the primary reasons

Photo 35. Mealing bins, *room 31, south pueblo, Raven Site Ruins. Showing the large bowl section that was re-used as a scoop to transfer the ground corn from one bin to the next.*

why many of the sherds are missing from the vessels. The prehistoric peoples in the Southwest re-used broken ceramic material in a variety of ways.

The principle re-use of broken ceramics was to grind the pieces up and add them as temper to new clay, to produce more vessels. This ground sherd temper is the most common temper that was used at Raven Site Ruins. The grinding and recycling of sherds back into new vessels probably accounts for the majority of missing ceramic material.

A large section of a broken bowl would often be re-used as a scoop. Large bowl sections have been discovered inside the mealing bins in the south pueblo. The corn was ground, and then scooped with the bowl fragment into the next, and finer, mealing bin. The rim of the bowl fragment and the broken edge often show tremendous wear from repeated use.

Broken bowls were also utilized as platters. It is interesting that the prehistoric potters rarely made plates. Bowls seem to have been the principle serving utensil. Plates are very rarely discovered in the ceramic assemblages. If the edge of the bowl was broken, and the bottom was intact, very often these would be ground down into platters

Photo 35a. Broken bowls that were ground down and used as platters. Occasionally, a broken jar would be re-used as a bowl.

or lids for other vessels.

When a ceramic container broke, it was not necessarily discarded or re-worked into something else. Very often the prehistoric potter would repair the damaged vessels. This was accomplished by drilling a hole on either side of the crack, and then binding the vessel together with a perishable material such as sinew. These repair holes are

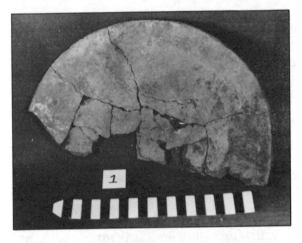

Photo 35b. Platters were created prehistorically, but they are only rarely discovered in the ceramic assemblages. Bowls seem to have been the principle serving utensil.

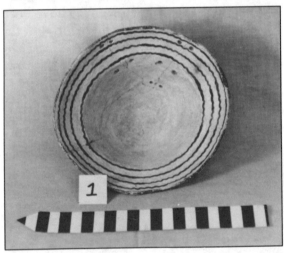

Photo 35c. Small bowl with multiple repair holes. To repair the crack, holes were drilled on either side and the pieces were tied together.

frequently found in prehistoric ceramic assemblages, although the material that was used to do the binding has not survived preservation.

Broken ceramics were ground into a variety of useful objects other than just temper. Large sherds were used as scrapers to form new vessels and shape the wet clay. These pottery scrapers are often just an irregular sherd that has been ground smooth on the edges.

Another object created from potsherds is identical to the scrapers, except that there is a notch at the top that has been ground into the edge. Most archaeologists consider these to be gaming pieces, or counting pieces, used while gambling much like our modern poker chips. This explanation does not, however, explain the notch. It could

Photo 35d. **Large sherds** *that have been ground smooth on the edges and were used prehistorically to scrape the coils from the wet clay during the production of other vessels.*

Photo 35e. Sherds *that are ground smooth on the edges. Most archaeologists conclude that these are gaming pieces, but offer no explanation for the notch.*

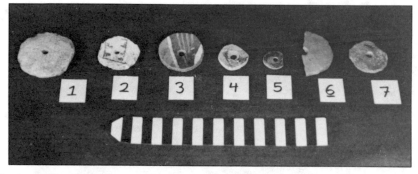

Photo 35f. **Whorls made from sherds.** *These were used to stabilize the shaft of pump and bow drills.*

be possible that these are in fact pottery scrapers for forming the wet clay, and that the notch was used to create the protruding rim of the bowl or jar.

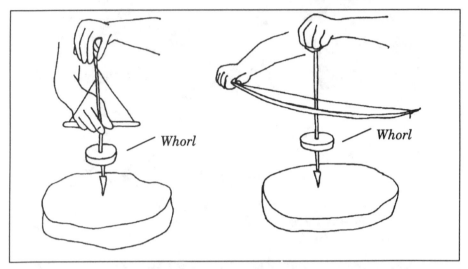

Figure 18. Pump drill and bow drill *with ceramic whorl at the center of the shaft. (From Barnett 73)*

Another prehistoric use for a potsherd was to grind it into a disk, drill a hole in the center, and use it as a stabilizer on the shaft of a bow drill or pump drill. These artifacts are called whorls (see Figure 18).

Very often in the ceramic assemblages, disks made from sherds will

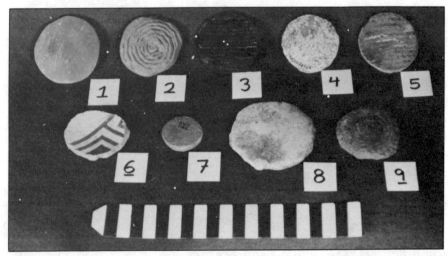

Photo 35g. Sherds *that have been cut into disks but have not yet been drilled.*

be found that have no center hole. It has been speculated that the larger of these were used as lids to jars and that the smaller ones are whorls that have not yet been drilled.

Smaller sherds are often ground and shaped into dice. One side will be painted and the other side plain. Several of these would be thrown at one time to achieve the bet. Sherds were also ground and shaped then drilled at the top with a very small hole. These were used as pendants and ornaments.

Photo 35h. *Sherds that were ground on the edges and shaped into dice. One side is painted and one plain. Several would be thrown at one time.*

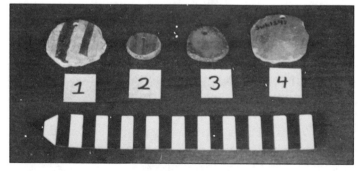

Photo 35i. *Sherds that have been shaped and drilled for use as pendants and ornaments.*

Chapter 12

Prehistoric Tools
for Making Ceramics

When a prehistoric potter sat down to create a vessel, she used an assortment of different tools. Many of these tools are very similar to the tools that are used today in the hand-forming of ceramics. Among the artifacts recovered from Raven Site Ruins, these potter's tools are frequently recovered. Often during the excavation of a room, we will recover the raw clay in large unfired chunks, piled in the corner of the room, patiently waiting to be formed into a vessel. We have also found unfired vessels that were formed and even painted, then left unfinished during the abandonment of the site.

In two different locations in the north pueblo at Raven Site Ruins, evidence of kilns has been discovered. One kiln discovered on the extreme north/east room block, was very similar to the modern Zuni bread ovens that can still be seen on the reservation today. This small beehive unit still contained an unfired vessel, centered in the oven, ready to fire.

Much of the pottery-making process focused on the grinding of sherds to produce a temper to add to the native clays. In other areas of the Southwest the prehistoric peoples used sand or a combination of sand and sherds. At Raven Site Ruins, almost all of the ceramics that were produced on the site contain a ground sherd temper. This is one of the first features of the ceramics that the archaeologist examines to determine if the vessel was locally produced or imported.

Pigments for slips and paints were also ground and mixed. The evidence of this grinding process can be seen in Photo 36. Mortars and pestles are a common discovery during excavations. Often traces of the pigments and minerals that were ground are still visible on the surface. Small vessels have also been discovered that still contain the ground powders. The natural mineral pieces that were used to create the pigment colors are also found with ground edges where powder has been removed during the grinding process.

Forming the clay at Raven Site Ruins was accomplished using the coil and scrape method. The potter would roll out long "snakes" of clay and coil these upward, creating the bottom of the vessel first, then the body and proceed toward the rim. At the bottom of many of the

Photo 36. Mortars and pestles *used to grind sherds into temper and colored minerals into pigments. Examples 2 and 9 still retain the ground turquoise pigment on the surface. Example 7 was used to grind iron ore into red slip pigment. Example 6 was used to grind the yellow pigment limonite and the small dish (Example 10) still contains the ground limonite powder.*

corrugated vessels the first coil is still visible. These coils were then scraped smooth using either an antelope rib or scapula scraper, or a sherd scraper. Many of the large shaped sherds that we have discovered at the site which appear to be either a pottery scraper or a counting or gaming piece, have a large notch ground in the edge. Other researchers consider these to be gaming pieces, but they offer no explanation for the notch, often explaining it as simply whimsical. It could be possible that these large shaped sherds are indeed pottery scrapers, and the notch could be used to form the rim of the bowl or jar. We have tested these pieces in this procedure and they work wonderfully well.

After the vessel is formed, it is polished using a small round river cobble. These polishing stones are also used after the surface slip is applied to polish the slip into the still damp clay. After the slip, the painted designs are created using a yucca brush. These unfortunately have not survived preservation at Raven Site Ruins.

Two other tools have been found at the site that may have been used in the production of ceramics. The first is a bone tool that has a cut zig-zag end. We tested this tool in wet clay and the impressions that were produced in the clay very much resemble many of the incised corrugations on the cooking vessels.

Another group of objects that have been the cause of much specu-
lation, are what appear to be clay plugs. These are made of the same
clay as was used in the production of ceramics. They are unfired.
Several of these have the impression of the top of an olla imbedded in
the plug, and they were obviously used to close the top of a jar at one
time. Closing the top of a jar during the production of the vessel may
have been done to slow drying, or these plugs could have sealed
finished ollas to protect the contents. Others of these clay plugs lack
this impression, and they are shaped to fit nicely in the hand. One
theory is that these were used while scraping the vessel to give the bowl
or jar some support from the inside during the scraping process.

If this is the case, then these artifacts are pottery anvils, which are
normally found in areas where ceramics were produced using a paddle
and anvil technique rather than the coil and scrape method. The
paddle and anvil technique is similar to the coil and scrape method,
except after the coils are formed into the vessel shape, they are
flattened using an anvil (usually made of stone) inside to support the
vessel, while a wooden paddle is applied to the outside. This technique
was used principally by the Hohokam cultural group whereas the coil
and scrape method is associated with the Anasazi and the Mogollon
peoples.

Photo 36a. Pottery making tools. (1) Various polishing stones. (2 and 3) Clay
plugs or anvils. (4) Sherd scrapers, one with a rim-forming notch. (5) Antelope
rib and scapula pottery scrapers. (6) A bone-incising tool used to create the
indented corrugated ceramics.

Chapter 13

The Ceramics of Raven Site Ruins & the Development of the Katsina Cult

There has recently been a great deal of research devoted to tracing the prehistoric development of the Katsina Cult. Much of this research has focused on the cultural changes that occurred between A.D. 1300 and A.D. 1400 and how these changes are reflected in the ceramic assemblages.

We have already noted, that after A.D. 1300 at Raven Site Ruins, there was a tremendous increase in the different types of ceramics that were produced. Two ceramic traditions continued side-by-side, the White Mountain Red Wares, and the Zuni Glaze Wares. We have partially accredited these changes with the introduction of the glaze paints around A.D. 1300, noting that the new glaze paint runs and blurs during firing. One group of potters liked the new colors that were produced with the glaze paints, and they went on to create the Zuni Glaze Ware series of pottery types. The other group of potters at Raven Site Ruins continued to use the older traditional paints, and they

Photo 37. Bowls that exhibit iconography relating to the introduction of the Katsina Cult at Raven Site Ruins. Example 1 demonstrates a thunderbird icon at center with cloud wings. Example 2 depicts a violent thunderstorm. Example 3 illustrates a thunderbird with cloud wings bringing rain to the village below. Katsina ceremonies were principally concerned with bringing rain. The Katsina spirits often travel as clouds.

created the later ceramic types in the White Mountain Red Ware sequence, terminating with Fourmile Polychrome around A.D. 1400.

From A.D.1300 to A.D. 1400 the list of ceramic types that were simultaneously produced at Raven Site Ruins is remarkable. These types include:

Wingate Polychrome	A.D. 1125 to A.D. 1200/1300
Wingate Black-on-red	A.D. 1125 to A.D. 1200/1300
St. Johns Black-on-red	A.D. 1175 to A.D. 1300
St. Johns Polychrome	A.D. 1175 to A.D. 1300
Tularosa Black-on-white	A.D. 1200 to A.D. 1300
Springerville Polychrome	A.D. 1250 to A.D. 1300
Pinedale Black-on-red	A.D. 1275 to A.D. 1325
Pinedale Polychrome	A.D. 1275 to A.D. 1325
Pinedale Black-on-white	A.D. 1275 to A.D. 1325
Cedar Creek Polychrome	A.D. 1300 to A.D. 1375
Heshotauthla Black-on-red	A.D. 1300 to A.D. 1400
Heshotauthla Polychrome	A.D. 1300 to A.D. 1400
Fourmile Polychrome	A.D. 1325 to A.D. 1400
Showlow Polychrome	A.D. 1325 to A.D. 1400
Kwakina Polychrome	A.D. 1325 to A.D. 1400
Pinnawa Polychrome	A.D. 1350 to A.D. 1450
Kechipawan Polychrome	A.D. 1375 to A.D. 1475

Notice the clustering of dates from A.D. 1300 to A.D. 1350+. This means that if someone lived at Raven Site Ruins between the years of A.D. 1300 and A.D. 1350 they would have had their choice of over seventeen different ceramic types. Why would any one pueblo have such a diversity of ceramics being produced at the same time?

One reason for such a diverse production of ceramics is an increase in trade. Raven Site Ruins are located in an area with abundant resources for ceramic production. There are several different local clay sources with a variety of colors that occur naturally. The minerals that were used to produce different pigment colors are also easily found just a short walk from the site and firewood is plentiful. The site is also located only a hundred yards from the Little Colorado River along the prehistoric Pochteca trade routes.

After A.D. 1300 Raven Site Ruins was at least one of the major ceramic production areas in the entire region. Several researchers have suggested that the White Mountain Red Wares were status items and that they were produced at only a few large sites (Lightfoot/Jewett 84). The ceramics that were produced on the site were traded over a very wide distribution area. This increase in trade also increased contact with other cultural groups. This increased contact resulted in the exchange of not only ceramics for other exotic goods, but ideas, songs, legends, stories and, possibly, the Katsina Cult, moved from one cultural area to the next. It is noted that with the introduction of the Katsina Cult around the year A.D. 1300, into a pueblo that previously did not practice the cult, there are increases in trade and exotic items appear in the cultural assemblages that seem to have arrived from the south. There are also increases in the size of the pueblos that adopted the cult. Room blocks are built to enclose a central plaza. This accommodates viewing the performance of Katsina rituals.

The south pueblo at Raven Site Ruins demonstrates all of the characteristics believed to be associated with the introduction of the Katsina Cult in the 14th century. The diverse ceramic assemblages indicate a rapid increase in trade. Ceramic types are found in the south pueblo that were produced to the south, below the Mogollon Rim and traded to the site, including: Gila Polychrome, Tonto Polychrome and several large plain ware ollas and jars. The room blocks in the south pueblo were built to enclose the central plaza. Previously on the site, the older north pueblo did not enclose the plaza. The plaza was located to the south of the room blocks. New construction after A.D. 1300 enclosed the plaza on three sides. This new construction increased the size of Raven Site Ruins from a pueblo with perhaps 300 rooms, to one with over 800. This is a dramatic populational increase.

The Katsina Cult is believed to have been introduced from Mexico between the years A.D. 1150 and A.D. 1400 (Carlson 70, Di Peso 74, Dutton 63, Hibben 66, Smith 52). Tracing the actual movement of the cult from one area is still debated, but one route suggested by Carlson and Di Peso late in the 1200s follows the San Pedro River Valley up to the Mogollon Rim and into the White Mountains. The introduction of the Cult to Raven Site Ruins would then have traveled northward, from Mexico, through the Salado Indian groups and eventually to the Upper Little Colorado areas. The presence of the exotic Salado ceramics at the south pueblo of Raven Site Ruins indicates that the new trade networks extended into the Salado areas following this route.

Ceramic evidence other than just type diversity suggests that the Katsina Cult was fully developed at Raven Site Ruins by no later than A.D. 1325. Beginning with the introduction of Pinedale Polychrome, evidence of Katsina-associated symbols begin to appear on the ceramics in the White Mountain area. As the Pinedale Style evolves into the Fourmile Style, Katsina figures and symbols are full blown and well-represented on the ceramic assemblages. The cult is well-established at Raven Site Ruins by certainly no later than A.D. 1350. Many researchers believe that the Fourmile ceramics were influenced by the

Kayenta-Tusayan (Hopi) ceramic types that were made to the north (Carlson 70, Adams 91). Fourmile Style is also found on contemporary prehistoric Hopi ceramics including Sikyatki Polychrome and Jeddito Black-on-yellow.

The Fourmile Style, and Katsina Cult symbols on ceramics, continues after A.D. 1400 and can be seen on Matsaki Polychrome and Matsaki Brown-on-buff. Matsaki Brown-on-buff has been found in large quantities in the south pueblo at Raven Site Ruins. The Matsaki ceramics are believed to be copies of the northern prehistoric Hopi Yellow-wares including Sikyatki Polychrome. This is further supported by the prehistoric potter's attempt to produce a yellow slip color which was never fully achieved. The buff tones were as close to the yellow as the potters were able to produce. There is clearly a shift in vessel form with the Matsaki Brown-on-buff ollas from Raven Site Ruins that further supports the idea that the Matsaki ollas are poor copies of the northern Hopi ceramics. The ollas are initially produced with the traditional globular body. Later, there is an attempt to produce a sharp "Gila Style" shoulder on the jar. This is even later followed by widening the shoulder to dramatic proportions and bringing it sharply to the bottom of the vessel. This produces a "flying saucer" shaped olla, a very similar form to those produced in the northern Hopi areas.

Raven Site Ruins exhibits all of the cultural changes between A.D. 1300 and A.D. 1400 that researchers recognize as being related to the arrival of the Katsina Cult during this period of prehistory. Meaningful symbols on the Fourmile ceramics are abundant from the site, and most of these represent Katsina-related ideas and information, primarily the bringing of rain, and spirits traveling in the form of clouds.

| *Example1* | *Example 2* | *Example 3* |

Photo 37a. *Matsaki Brown-on-buff ollas demonstrating the transition from the original globular bodied olla, Ex. 1, then later to a sharp "Gila" shoulder, Ex. 2 and at last to the very large shoulder area, Ex. 3, which creates a "flying saucer" shaped jar. This saucer shape copies the northern prehistoric Hopi ceramic styles.*

Chapter 14

Symbols: Meaningful Icons Painted on the Ceramics from Raven Site Ruins

In the summer of 1990 during the analysis of ceramic material from the Raven Site Ruins, a Fourmile Polychrome bowl grew out of the surface of the lab table. It illustrated a narrative. This vessel, SW1391a, caused quite a debate. The bowl is unquestionably authentic. It was excavated from the floor of room #20. Room #20 was occupied around A.D. 1380 to 1400 and possibly even after A.D. 1400, dates somewhat later than the presence of Fourmile ceramics would indicate. However, it is believed that vessel SW1391a was manuported from the north pueblo, near datums 4 and 5, and was retained by the south pueblo inhabitants as an heirloom piece. It is believed that the Fourmile material found on the entire site, including the Fourmile ceramics that are found in the south pueblo, room #20, and vessel SW1391a, were produced by the women of the north pueblo toward the end of the White Mountain Red Ware ceramic production.

Vessel SW1391a exhibits all of the Fourmile Polychrome ceramic characteristics such as black banding lines edged in white kaolin etc., and the bowl is clearly typical of the ceramic type, but what startled curators when the bowl was assembled after cleaning, was the interior design. On the bowl interior is the depiction of a thunderbird flying over a pueblo below. The representation was remarkable because it was graphic enough to easily recognize the nature of the story being depicted, however, the bird and the pueblo were composed of symbolic units with specific meanings. These units could then be compared with other vessels and aid in other translations.

It was not the depiction of the thunderbird which at first caused excitement, but instead, the representation of the pueblo below the bird. It was in fact, several months before the pueblo glyph was recognized. The vessel sat on a lab shelf gathering dust, a beautiful Fourmile, with a wonderful depiction of a thunderbird. Thunderbirds are well represented throughout prehistoric pueblo peoples ceramic production. They are also abundantly encountered on the rock art of the Southwest. Thunderbirds are easy to recognize. The icon was unquestionably important to the people who produced the glyph. The thunderbird depicted on SW1391a is of particular interest because of the combination of symbolic elements used to produce the bird, including an arrow point head with water dots, cloud wings to bring the rains, and a rain streamer trailing behind the bird.

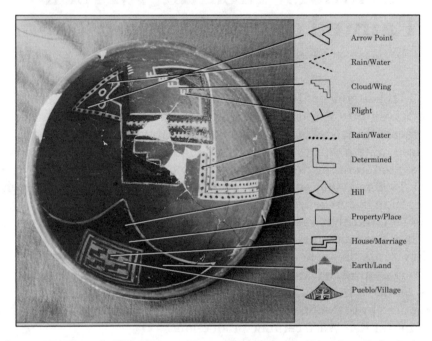

Photo 38. Vessel SW1391a. Fourmile Polychrome bowl depicting a thunderbird bringing rain to the village below. This depiction, and the meaningful symbols that it employs, reflect the development of the Katsina Cult in the White Mountains of Arizona.

The representation of the pueblo below the bird is composed of four elemental units. The outline of the glyph is roughly an equal lateral triangle which represents the "hill" upon which the village is built. Contained inside the triangle is a square containing interlocked terraced units. The square represents "geographical place", i.e., property, house, garden, etc., and in this case the pueblo itself which is composed of many houses. These "houses" are further represented in the glyph by the interlocked terraced units inside the square. There are four interlocked units in all, that is, "more than one". Filling the area outside the square and inside the triangle are rows of parallel lines representing "earth/land". These parallel lines could represent crop rows. One is reminded of the "straight furrow" pattern used in quilting. It may be argued that the prehistoric pueblo people who produced this bowl may not have planted their crops in rows, however, they did irrigate, and irrigation is conducive to planting in an ordered manner.

Also crops were planted outside the immediate village as represented in the glyph. If the interpretation of the pueblo glyph is correct, then five elemental units or icons have been discovered:

 "hill", the triangular enclosure surrounding the total glyph.

 "human created space", represented by the square unit inside the triangle.

 "house / marriage", (four individual units) represented by the interlocked terraced units found inside the square.

 "earth / land", represented by the parallel lines around the outside of the square and within the triangle.

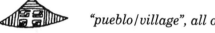 *"pueblo / village", all of the above.*

If this analysis of the "pueblo" glyph found on vessel SW1391a is correct then several options appear, the most exciting being that basic unit icons have unit meaning which should be constant at least for the temporal period of this ceramic type's production. Other Fourmile vessels should exhibit similar icon use, possibly even the same use of the same symbols. Because these symbols are found on ceramics, instead of something more difficult to date such as the rock art of the Southwest, then we can assign a temporal span for the icons' introduction, use and disuse prehistorically. Because the "pueblo" glyph is composed of several unit icons in combination, it is possible to seek out other "pueblo" glyphs on other vessels for comparison. Variations in the form of the glyph should be expected, however, the "pueblo" icon should retain a majority of the basic units.

Other vessels sharing the combination of icons that may represent "pueblo" were sought in The White Mountain Archaeological Center's collections from the Raven Site Ruins and from across the country in the repositories held by museums and other institutions. The literature was also re-examined for representations of the five icons discovered. Several other examples of the "pueblo" icon were found in the White Mountain Archaeological Center's collections and one remarkable representation was found in J.W. Fewkes "Designs on Prehistoric Hopi Pottery" printed in 1895. The Fewkes example is particularly interesting, because the bowl illustrated displays an identical narrative to vessel SW1391a. The two vessels may have overlapped temporally, but they were produced several hundred miles apart. The Fewkes example is a Sikyatki, basically a Jeddito, coal-fired from near the present day town of Polaka on Second Mesa. Undoubtedly produced by the ancestors of the Hopi. SW1391a is a Fourmile Polychrome, from a site where the producers of the Fourmile Polychromes migrated from the site, sometime after A.D. 1380. Some researchers believe that both the Fourmile Polychromes and the Hopi Yellow-wares were produced contemporaneously, others feel that the Fourmile Polychromes temporally preceded the Hopi Yellow-wares. Both types probably overlap in time.

The similarity between the glyphs on these two vessels may at first be difficult to recognize. Only after the entire vessel, in both cases, is examined and interpreted are the similarities clear. In the Fewkes example, "Bird With Double Eyes", the "pueblo" icon is represented below the thunderbird in a very similar way to vessel SW1391a. Once again the "hill" icon is present as a triangle surrounding the entire glyph. Within the triangle "hill" there are interlocked terraced units representing "house/marriage", these are surrounded by the square "property/geographic place" icon and the parallel lines representing "earth/land" are found above and below the interlocked terraced units. All of the elements of the combined icon "pueblo" are present and they are arranged in a very similar manner to the Fourmile example from Raven Site Ruins. Both vessels, upon translation, depict a protectorate thunderbird bringing rain to the pueblo below. These vessels undoubtedly reflect the development of the Katsina Cult. The Fourmile

Figure 19. "Bird With Double Eyes". The hourglass body shape of the bird is interesting. This may indicate "starvation", "war", or it may even be another "water" icon as found in the water gourd form. (From Fewkes 1895)

Polychrome ceramics are the first in the White Mountains to ignore the traditional symmetry of earlier wares. The asymmetrical layouts are probably the result of painting meaningful combinations of symbols, rather than mere aesthetics. Most researchers feel that Pinedale Polychrome ceramics, which appear somewhat earlier begin to show evidence of the Katsina Cult. With the later development of the Fourmile Polychromes, the Cult is full blown.

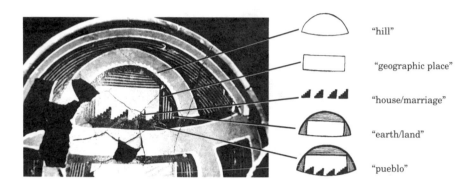

Photo 38a Vessel SW1012, Fourmile Polychrome bowl with the "pueblo" glyph. The terraced units in this example are repeated in profile but not interlocked, unless the white negative background constitutes the interlocked combination. (White Mountain Archaeological Center Collections)

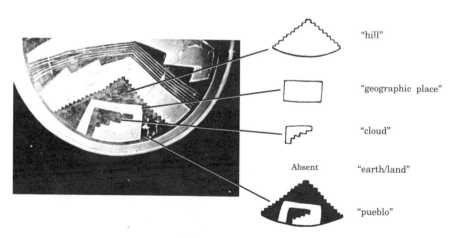

Photo 38b. Vessel Pi 2. Fourmile Polychrome. This "pueblo" example contains at center a large "cloud" icon, probably representing a place name, i.e., "cloud pueblo" or the "cloud clan." (White Mountain Archaeological Center Collections)

With the discovery of several examples of the "pueblo" glyph found on many ceramic types separated spatially and temporally, it may therefore be possible to trace the appearance, use and disuse of the icon over space and time.

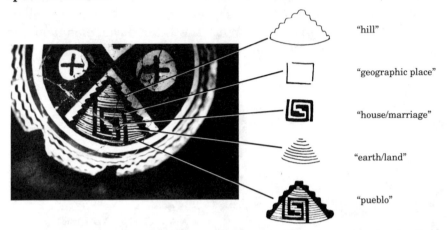

"hill"

"geographic place"

"house/marriage"

"earth/land"

"pueblo"

Photo 38c. Vessel Pi 5. Gila Polychrome bowl. *In this example, the "earth / land" icon runs throughout the center of the glyph. (White Mountain Archaeological Center Collections)*

Chart I

Variations of the "pueblo" glyph.

SW1391a.

....

Fewkes.

....

Pi 5.

....

SW1012.

....

Pi 2.

....

Granted, not all of the "pueblo" glyphs exhibit all of the individual elements defined with the discovery of SW1391a. The Pi 2 example lacks the "earth/land" icon and contains only a single terraced unit at center. These variations temporally and spatially should be expected. Certain elements of the basic glyph may be irrelevant to the particular pueblo being represented. With each depiction, different information concerning the pueblo is being represented, which in many cases, leaves only room in the finite space of the vessel for that information and little extra. This would mean that some of the basic units we have classified as being relevant to the "pueblo" glyph must be reduced in order to include other information, leaving just enough of the pueblo glyph intact to be recognized. This is best illustrated with a sherd excavated from the Raven Site Ruins which is part of a Tularosa olla dating between A.D. 1200 and A.D. 1300. The sherd is part of the shoulder area of the olla and it contains a pueblo glyph in a reduced form. In this example, the glyph was reduced to accommodate the small size of the representation. The triangular "hill" icon is present, also the square "geographical place" and the "earth/land". Inside the square "geographical place" icon there are three dots instead of the usual terraced units. With such a small "pueblo" representation, the terraced units, i.e., "house/marriage", were reduced to simply dots, that is, "more than one" of something, presumably houses as would have been illustrated by terraced units if the example had been larger.

Photo 38d. Tularosa sherd, R-17, Raven Site Ruin.

By recognizing the basic pueblo glyph and its variations, it is then possible to focus on those variations and ascertain their individual meanings, noting which are a part of the basic pueblo depiction, and which are relating information about the individual pueblo being depicted. In the example above, the sherd from room #17 showing the three dots at center could be representing "house/marriage" by the dots, as would be expected in a larger representation, but the information that the glyph contains says simply "three of something", or "more than one".

With the basic units of the pueblo glyph understood, it is possible to cross check these basic units against other glyphs found in ceramic and on rock art depictions.

Chart II

Prehistoric Icons from the Ceramics of the White Mountains

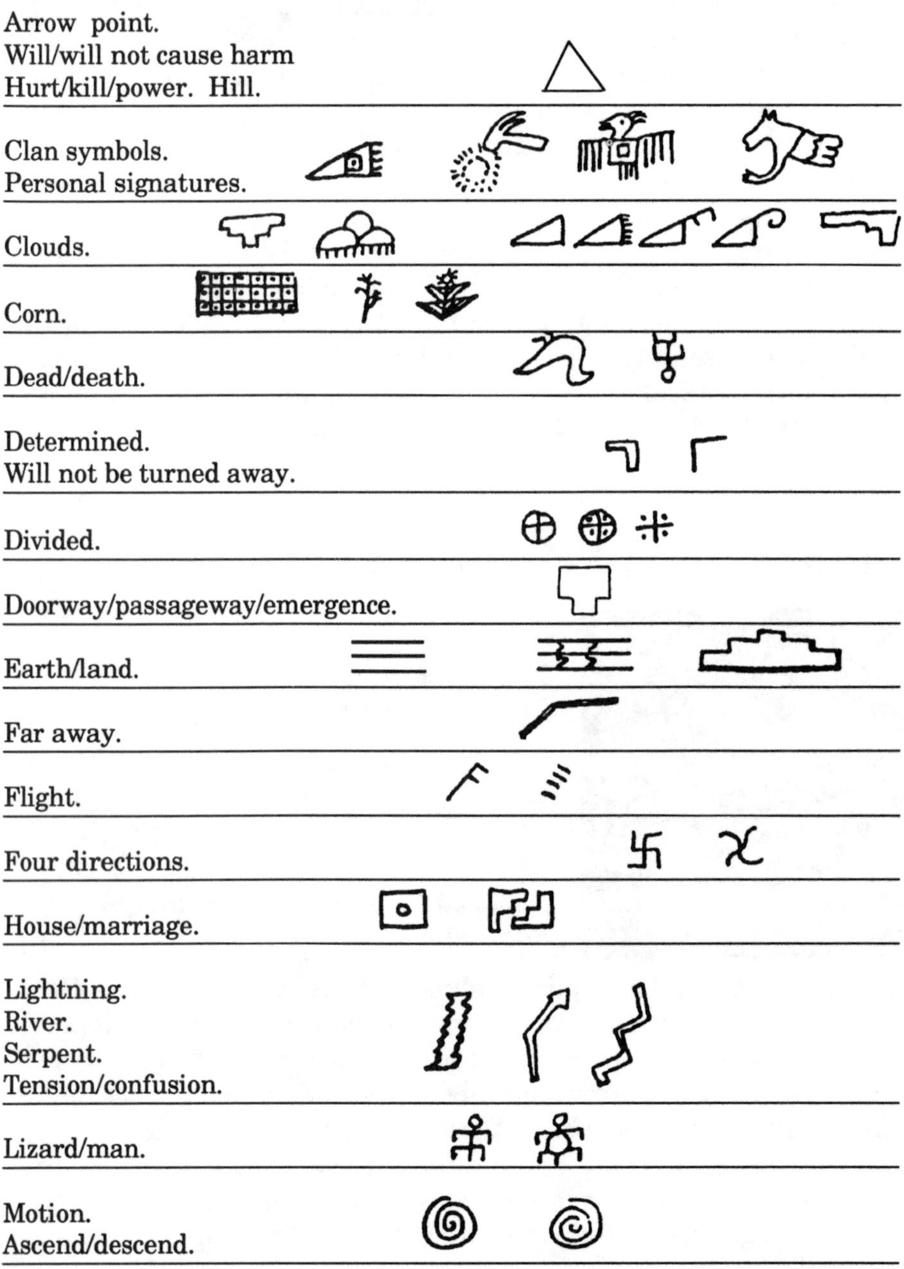

Arrow point. Will/will not cause harm Hurt/kill/power. Hill.	
Clan symbols. Personal signatures.	
Clouds.	
Corn.	
Dead/death.	
Determined. Will not be turned away.	
Divided.	
Doorway/passageway/emergence.	
Earth/land.	
Far away.	
Flight.	
Four directions.	
House/marriage.	
Lightning. River. Serpent. Tension/confusion.	
Lizard/man.	
Motion. Ascend/descend.	

(Continued next page)

(Chart II continued)

Mountain/hill.			
Night sky/day sky.			
Property/geographic place.			
Pueblo/village.			
Safety/peace.			
Siege.			
Sky.		Sky	Earth
Smoke.			
Something there.			
War.			
Water/rain. Falling rain.			
Wind.			

Chart II is a summary of all of the individual icons that have been discovered during this research. Many of these symbols and their meanings have long been recognized, others are new. Some of these new symbol interpretations may be wrong. Every attempt has been made to stay within the parameters of the data so far discovered.

With this expanded list of symbols, it is now possible to see more on the surface of Southwest ceramics than "just pretty patterns" and for the first time in centuries, many of these vessels will again be able to tell their stories.

For a complete analysis icon by icon, their meanings and how each symbol was isolated and translated see "Talking Pots, Deciphering the Symbols of a Prehistoric People" (Cunkle 93) in the bibliography.

Chapter 15

The Ceramic Spirit Break

Found throughout the ceramic assemblage of the Southwest is a design element known as the "spirit break". This consists of a band which encircles the vessel, usually around the neck of ollas or the interior of bowls. This band has a single break, or gap. This break or gap in the band is known as the "spirit break" of the vessel. It allows the spirit of the vessel to escape without the necessity of actually smashing the piece. This "spirit break" is called the "onane" by the Zuni. It is a road to life, a way to emerge from the sipapu.

The spirit break can still be found today on many of the modern ceramics being produced by Native Americans and occasionally on Navajo weavings.

Throughout prehistory, ritual "killing" of ceramics and other artifacts has been performed, often associated with the burial of the artifact with the dead. In many cases this ritual killing is performed by the total destruction of the artifact and then the remaining pieces are also interred. This ritual killing of the ceramic vessel is not entirely limited to grave offerings. Cushing observed a ceremony during his stay with the Zuni in the 19th century where the katsina clowns would go from house to house and smash vessels of the finest quality. These vessels were purposely left outside the rooftop doorways to accommodate the clowns. Many of the highest quality White Mountain Red Wares that are found at Raven Site Ruins are splattered over a wide provenance of the site. This may be explained by a similar prehistoric ceremony as was observed by Cushing in the late 1800s (Cushing 80-81).

Rather than totally destroying the grave offerings, many groups chose to remove only a small piece or area of the object before burying the same with their deceased. The most notable examples are the "kill holes" found on the center bottom of Mimbres bowls. The bowl is placed over the face of the deceased, and the bottom of the bowl is punched out to allow the spirit of the vessel to escape. This leaves the bowl basically intact. Other examples of the ritual killing of ceramics is to break off a small area of the rim of the bowl or jar before the burial is performed. Photo 39c shows three small Gila Polychrome bowls that are similarly rim-mutilated. Grinding or notching the edge of the bowl is another form of "killing" the vessel before internment. All of the above examples express the same rationale. The spirit of the vessel must emerge/be able to leave/move/travel/escape, i.e., pass from one place to another. The smashing of the vessel accommodates this need, as does rim mutilation, as does the spirit break painted on the rim or neck of the ceramics. The painted ceramic spirit breaks create a doorway for the spirit of the vessel to move from the realm of this world to the next level of existence in pueblo thought.

Photo 39. Snowflake Black-on-white olla and Matsaki Brown-on-buff ollas both with spirit breaks encircling the neck. The ends of the spirit break on both employ the unilateral terrace which is a cloud representation.

Photo 39a. Example 1, Tularosa Black-on-white olla top with spirit break encircling the neck. Example 2, Pinnawa Glaze-on-white bowl with a spirit break in the center of the vessel. Notice the blurring of the glaze paint.

Photo 39b. Example 1, Gila Polychrome bowl *with a spirit break near the rim. The flaring of the rim is a classic Gila Polychrome form.* ***Example 2, Fourmile Polychrome bowl glue-up*** *with a predominate spirit break employing the unilateral cloud symbol.*

Photo 39c. Three small Gila/Pinto Polychrome bowls *with deliberate rim mutilation.*

Photo 39d. Mimbres bowls *with the ritual kill hole at bottom center.*

Chapter 16

Synonyms to Ceramic Type Names

(What we call them and what other researchers have called them before)

Throughout this text, we have referred to different ceramic types by a type name. The type name that has been used is the currently applied "handle" for that particular ceramic type. However, this taxonomy is constantly changing and has been for over a century. It is therefore necessary to list the synonyms for all of the ceramics that we have discussed. Many of these previous type names are more descriptive than they are nomenclature. This is because many of the early researchers who were the first to encounter a new ceramic type simply described the new ceramic with a sentence or two rather than boldly name a new type. Here at Raven Site Ruins, when we discover a new type or a type variant, we fondly apply a name that may or may not survive the scrutiny of academia, such as "Kwakina Not-quite-so-polychrome", "Kwakina Polychrome-plus", and "Raven Polychrome". Our job is research, not semantics.

When I attended the ceramic conference in Flagstaff, Arizona in 1993, I heard many of these archaic type names applied in an attempt to describe newly discovered variants and types. It is important to recognize the similarities to similar ceramics. However, falling back on less literature rather than relying on the current information, even if it is unpublished, is weak.

The following is a list of AKA's, that you will need if you stumble upon something that was written early in the twentieth century.

PUERCO BLACK-ON-RED AKA:
North Plains Black-on-red, in part	(Olson/Wasley 56)
Little Colorado Ware, in part	(Roberts 32)
Black-on-red, found at Chaco, in part,	(Hawley 50)

(Continued next page . . .)

(Continued from previous page . . .)

WINGATE POLYCHROME AKA:
Querino Polychrome/Houck Polychrome	(Colton/Hargrave 37)
	(Hawley 50)
	(Martin/Willis 40)
	(Olson/Wasley 56)
	(Rinaldo 59)
Houck Ware	(Roberts 32)
Springerville Polychrome	(Martin/Rinaldo/Barter57)
	(Danson 57)
Little Colorado Type	(Roberts 32)
St. Johns Polychrome, in part,	(Kidder/Shepard 36)

WINGATE BLACK-ON-RED AKA:
Little Colorado Black-on-red Ware	(Hawley 29)
Two Color Painted Ware	(Spier 19)
North Plains Black-on-red, in part	(Olson/Wasley 56)
Little Colorado Ware, in part	(Roberts 32)

ST. JOHNS BLACK-ON-RED AKA:
Black-on-orange Red	(Haury/Hargrave 31)
Little Colorado Black-on-red, in part	(Hargrave 29)
Wingate Black-on-red, in part	(Martin/Willis 40)
Tularosa Black-on-red	(Mera 34/ Martin/Willis 40)

ST. JOHNS POLYCHROME AKA:
Three color painted ware	(Spier 19)
Black and White-on-red	(Spier 17)
Little Colorado Black-on-red	(Hargrave 29)
Little Colorado Polychrome	(Haury/Hargrave 31)
Chevlon Ware	(Hough 30)
Springerville Polychrome, in part	(Olson 59/Danson 57)

SPRINGERVILLE POLYCHROME AKA:
Little Colorado Polychrome, in part	(Haury/Hargrave 31)

PINEDALE POLYCHROME AKA:
Proto-fourmile Polychrome	(Haury 30)
Red Ware	(Fewkes 04)
Chevlon Ware	(Hough 30)
Three color glazed and painted Ware	(Spier 19)

PINEDALE BLACK-ON-RED AKA:
Pinedale Polychrome, in part	(Haury 32)

CEDAR CREEK POLYCHROME AKA:
Fourmile Polychrome, in part	(Martin/Willis 40)

(Continued next page . . .)

(Continued from previous page . . .)

    Transitional Polychrome   (Smiley 52)
    Pinedale Polychrome, in part   (Martin/Willis 40)
    Showlow Polychrome, in part   (Colton/Hargrave 37)
    Pinedale Fourmile Polychrome   (Wheat 52)

FOURMILE POLYCHROME AKA:
    Three color glazed and painted Ware (Spier 19)
    Red Ware   (Fewkes 04)

    Chevlon Ware   (Hough 30)
    White-bordered-Black-on-red   (Schmidt 28)
    Showlow Polychrome, in part   (Colton/Hargrave 37)
    Willow Mountain Polychrome   (Second Southwestern
                                      Ceramic Seminar 59)

SHOWLOW POLYCHROME AKA:
    Fourmile Polychrome, in part   (Haury/Hargrave 31/34)

POINT OF PINES POLYCHROME AKA:
    Fourmile Polychrome, Point of
        Pines Variety   (Wendorf 50)

HESHOTAUTHLA POLYCHROME AKA:
    Heshota Polychrome   (Carlson 70)
    Black-and-white Paint-on-red, in part (Spier 17)
    Bowls of thin red or orange-red ware,
        ornamented interiorly, in black or dark
        green glaze, and externally, in white
        non-glaze   (Hodge 20)
    Type II   (Hodge 24)
    Type B, Black or green glaze-on-red
        or orange-red.   (Hodge 23)
    Heshotauthla Glaze Polychrome   (Reed 55)

HESHOTAUTHLA BLACK-ON-RED AKA:
    Pinnawa Black-on-red   (Colton/Hargrave 37)
    Type II, red or orange, sometimes
        fired to brownish or greyish,
        ornamented usually in geometric
        patterns in black or green glaze. (Hodge 24)
    Type B. Black or green glaze on red
        or orange-red   (Hodge 23)

KWAKINA POLYCHROME AKA:
    Glaze III, red outside with white
        within.   (Hodge 24)
    Wallace Polychrome   (Colton/Hargrave 37)

(Continued next page . . .)

(Continued from previous page . . .)

    Adamana Polychrome   (Colton/Hargrave 37)
    Pinnawa Polychrome, in part   (Colton/Hargrave 37)
    Kwakina Glaze Polychrome   (Reed 55)

PINNAWA GLAZE-ON-WHITE AKA:
    Hawikuh Glaze C, or Black, green, or
    purplish glaze on white or creamy
       slip.   (Hodge 23)
    White and Green Ware   (Fewkes 04)
    White Ware   (Hough 03)
    Hawikuh Glaze-on-white   (Colton/Hargrave 37)
    Black Glaze-on-white   (Hodge 20)
    Type III, All over white slip,
        ornamented both inside and outside
        with glaze   (Hodge 24)
    Two-color glaze Ware, white   (Spier 17)
    Glaze Ware, black-on-white   (Spier 17)

KECHIPAWAN POLYCHROME AKA:
    Pinnawa Glaze-Polychrome   (Reed 55)
    Arauca Polychrome   (Colton/Hargrave 37)
    Glaze D   (Hodge 23)
    Type IV   (Hodge 24)

MATSAKI BROWN-ON-BUFF AKA:
    Hawikuh Brown-on-buff   (Colton, unpublished
                                   notes)

TULAROSA BLACK-ON-WHITE AKA:
    Upper Gila Black-on-white   (Haury 31)

PINTO POLYCHROME AKA:
    Polychrome Red   (Kidder 24)
    Lower Gila Polychrome   (Kidder 24)
    Central Gila Polychrome   (Schmidt 28)
    Early Middle Gila Polychrome   (Hawley 29)

GILA POLYCHROME AKA:
    Polychrome Red   (Kidder 24)
    Lower Gila Polychrome   (Kidder 24)
    Central Gila Polychrome   (Schmidt 28)
    Early Middle Gila Polychrome   (Hawley 29)

TONTO POLYCHROME AKA:
    Lower Gila Polychrome   (Kidder 24)
    Central Gila Polychrome   (Schmidt 28)
    Early Middle Gila Polychrome   (Hawley 29)

Glossary

Absolute: In regard to assigning a date to prehistoric artifacts. An absolute date is one that is obtained by knowing a fixed rate of change that can be measured in regard to the artifact. Carbon 14 dating, dendrochronology, and obsidian hydration are examples of absolute dating techniques.

A.D.: Latin, anno domini, in the year of our Lord. Used to designate time, for example, "A.D. 1200" means that the event occurred 1200 years after the birth of Christ in the year 0. B.C. dates count backwards from the year 0. 1200 B.C. would refer a time 1200 years before the birth of Christ. One other abbreviation that you will sometimes encounter is B.P., which simply means "before the present". The B.P. dates are used when presenting C-14 dating evidence.

Anasazi: A Navajo word meaning "alien ancient one" sometimes interpreted to mean "ancient enemy". Basketmaker/pueblo culture of the plateau area of northern Arizona, New Mexico, Utah and Colorado. Contemporaneous with the Mogollon and Hohokam culture areas to the south and west.

Ahaiyuta: Zuni war twin, brother of Matsailema. According to Zuni legend, these brothers killed the monster Atahsaia, beheaded and disemboweled him and flung the head into the heavens where it became the lying star. The entrails became the Milky Way.

Amerindian: Any Native American Indian cultural group that inhabits or has inhabited the Americas, north or south.

Anthromorphic: Anthro refers to "man" and morphic "change". This term refers to any representation that resembles the human form. The term Zoomorphic is any representation that resembles an animal.

Apache: From the Zuni word "apachu" or "enemy". Group of tribes forming the most southern group of the Athapaskan speakers.

Archaeoastronomy: Research area of Archaeology that examines prehistoric correlations with astronomy or celestial events.

Archaeomagnetic: A dating technique which employs the use of fired clay that has not been moved from where it was fired. The bottoms of hearths in the floors of rooms at a prehistoric site can often be used to obtain a date using this technique. Iron particles in the clay freeze into a fixed magnetic north position during firing. Magnetic north wanders over time. By comparing the difference between the frozen iron particles' "north" orientation, and magnetic north today, a date can be determined when the last firing of the hearth occurred.

Areola: Small border or defined area. In ceramic analysis the areola refers to the border around the neck of a jar or olla. Tularosa ollas dating A.D. 1200 to A.D. 1300 often have a raised area around the neck of the olla. This raised areola is diagnostic of the pottery type.

Artistry: In ceramic description and analysis, artistry refers to the quality of execution and brush work of the painted designs.

Atahsaia: Zuni monster of legend that was beheaded and disemboweled by the warrior twins. His head and entrails were thrown into the sky. The head became the lying star. His entrails became the Milky Way.

Athapaskan: Native American Indian group, speakers of the Athapaskan language which consists of three major dialectic areas. This language group includes the Navajo and Apache. The Athapaskans arrived quite late into the Southwest, after A.D. 1500.

B.C.: See A.D.

B.P.: See A.D.

Carbon 14: An absolute dating technique using any sample that had been alive, and measuring the remaining C-14 in the sample by burning.

Casas Grandes: Large prehistoric trade center located in the Chihuahuan area of Mexico. Occupied as early as A.D. 1060 and lasting until about A.D. 1340. This pueblo produced a variety of trade items including lost wax cast copper bells and live parrots.

Cedar Creek: A White Mountain Red Ware ceramic type. Polychrome, using red slip, and black and white interior and exterior paints. Produced from A.D. 1300 to A.D. 1375.

Ceramic Types: A style of pottery, usually designated as a type based on color, form, temper, and spacial and temporal distribution.

Ceremonial: A system of formal rules enjoined by law, for observance in religious worship.

Cibola White Wares: Black-on-white ceramics from the Cibola region.

Corrugated: Regarding ceramics, vessels that were used for cooking. These jars have indentations or corrugations encompassing the outside of the vessel. This rough surface is believed to have aided in the transfer of heat, or to have prevented cracking during the heating and re-heating of the pot during the cooking procedure.

Crab Nebula: A star that exploded in the Taurus system in the year A.D. 1054. The star was visible in the daylight sky for 23 days. This was recorded by Chinese astronomers and a possible depiction appears on Mimbres pottery.

Cuneiform: Prehistoric Mesopotamian written language which used a reed stylus and wet clay tablet. Invented by the Sumerians about 3200 B.C.

Cultural Areas: Regional distribution of a particular set of cultural traits, i.e., specific ceramics, architecture, stone tools, language etc. that are unique to one group of people. The three main cultural areas found in the prehistoric Southwest are the Anasazi, Mogollon and Hohokam.

Dating Techniques: Various methods used to establish/assign a calendar date to an artifact or event prehistorically. These methods include stratigraphy, carbon 14, dendrochronology, pollen analysis, ceramic typology, potassium/argon, obsidian hydration, desert varnish measurement and archaeomagnetic measurements.

Dendrochronology: Tree-ring dating technique developed by astronomer A. E. Douglass, used primarily in the Southwest. The widths of tree rings vary depending upon the growth cycles, wet years, dry years and other conditions. By tracking the growth rings from the present into the past, a sequence of ring widths has been established. By comparing a prehistoric wood or charcoal sample with an unknown date to this sequence it is often possible to determine what year the tree was cut.

Desert Varnish: A naturally occurring discoloration on rocks of the Southwest. Produced on the surface of the stone over long periods of time due to moisture, seepage and the natural minerals in the rock. It is this varnish that was pecked or chiseled away to produce petroglyphs. There have been recent attempts to date petroglyphs by measuring desert varnish layers.

Determinatives: Also "key signs". In the evolution of written languages, determinatives or key signs appear, usually without a spoken value, but indicating important information such as "more than one", similar to the way we indicate plurals in English usually by adding an "s". Determinatives are used in a variety of ways. On the vessels presented in this study, determinatives are used to indicate emphasis, and to indicate which glyphs are to be read together.

Emblem: A visible sign of an idea. An object, or figure of an object, symbolizing another object or idea by natural aptness or association.

Ethnology: Science that deals with man, his origins, distributions, relations, and with the peculiarities that characterized different groups. The comparative and analytical study of cultures.

Field of Decoration: Area of a vessel that displays the painted designs. Vessel decoration fields are determined by the form of the vessel, for example, a bowl interior is one field of design, and the bowl exterior is another. Jars are often treated as one field of design.

Fire Clouding: An isolated field of discoloration found on the surface of prehistoric ceramics caused by firing.

Form: In regard to ceramics, the shape of a vessel.

Fourmile: A White Mountain Red Ware ceramic type, dating A.D. 1325 to A.D. 1400. A Polychrome, this type exhibits the height of iconography use in the White Mountains. Bowls and jars are slipped red on the interior and exterior and black and white paint are used on both surfaces.

Fourmile Style: A collection of characteristics painted on prehistoric pottery that dates between A.D. 1325 and A.D. 1400 including the introduction of asymmetrical motifs. The entire bowl interior was used as a field of design. Fourmile Style is believed to be a reflection of the developing Katsina Cult in the White Mountains of Arizona.

Framing Lines: A line that encloses a motif, pattern, or field of design. A banding line is a framing line which encloses an entire field of design.

Gila: Ceramic type produced primarily below the Mogollon Rim in Arizona, dating A.D. 1300+. Examples in this study are Polychromes, with red slipped exteriors and black-on-white interiors in the case of bowls.

Hachuring: Lines used to fill a space. These lines may be parallel to the unit they fill, or they may oppose the unit. Often they are diagonal to the unit. The width of the hachure lines, how fine they are created, and their orientation to the unit they fill are all recognized as diagnostic to the differentiation of various ceramic types and styles.

Heshotauthla: A Zuni Glaze Ware polychrome pottery found in the White Mountains of Arizona. Vessels are slipped red on the interior and exterior, black paint is vitreous, white is chalky and kaolin. This type dates from A.D. 1275 to A.D. 1300.

Hieroglyphs: A picture script of the ancient Egyptian priesthood. It is believed that hieroglyphs became a flowing realistic/graphic form of writing aided by the media of papyrus.

Hohokam: Prehistoric Cultural group who arrived in the Southwest from Mexico and occupied the areas around Phoenix, Arizona and as far north as Flagstaff. Contemporaneous with the Anasazi and Mogollon cultural groups. Hohokam culture exhibits many unique traits such as paddle and anvil ceramic construction, the use of ball courts, extensive irrigation, and unusual lithic material such as paint pallets.

Holbrook Style: A unique ceramic style that was used on a variety of ceramic types from A.D. 1000 to A.D. 1150. consisting of solid motifs only.

Hopi: A pueblo people of northeastern Arizona. Possible ancestors of the prehistoric pueblo groups. A very esoteric society with practicing Katsina Cults.

Hukangwaa: A Hopi storm god who assisted the war twins after a smoking test.

Icon/iconography: Illustrations of a subject by pictures or other representations. A recognized unit.

Janus Face: An anthromorphic representation found on both Mimbres and Casas Grandes ceramics which depicts the human face with gnashing teeth and a triangular fleshless nose. Possibly a "death" symbol.

Katsina: An ancestral spirit of the pueblo peoples believed to visit the pueblos at seasonal ceremonies, traveling in the form of clouds, usually to bring rain.

Kaolin: A white chalky paint found on prehistoric ceramics, especially the White Mountain Red Wares.

Key Signs: See "Determinatives".

Kiva: A ceremonial chamber. Kivas come in all shapes and sizes including round, rectangular, square and D-shaped. Entrance and lighting usually from the roof, usually includes an altar, hearth and sipapu.

Kokopelli: The humpbacked flute player. Depictions are found abundantly on the rock art of the Southwest and occasionally on ceramics. The exact nature of this deity is unknown. The humpback often resembles a backpack full of seeds. Kokopelli often proudly exhibits an erection.

Kwakina: A ceramic type. Zuni Glaze Ware. Bowls are slipped red outside and white inside. Black glaze paint inside, and white and black outside. Produced between A.D. 1325 and A.D. 1400.

Layout: The organization of the field of decoration of ceramic vessels.

Lug: In reference to prehistoric ceramics, the addition of formed clay to accommodate straps or handles, usually found on canteens or jars. Lugs are often in the form of zoomorphs. Finger lugs on smaller vessels are commonly found on Tularosa ceramics dating between A.D. 1200 and A.D. 1300, at Raven Site Ruins.

Mano: A stone held in the hand, used in grinding against a metate.

Matsailema: One of the Zuni war twins.

Matsaki Polychrome: A Zuni ceramic type dating between A.D. 1475 and A.D. 1600.

Metate: A large platform stone used in grinding.

Midden: A prehistoric trash pile.

Mimbres: Prehistoric cultural subgroup of the Mogollon, located in southwestern New Mexico. Most noted for black-on-white bowls exhibiting graphic anthromorphic and zoomorphic depictions. These vessels were primarily used as mortuary offerings.

Mogollon: Prehistoric cultural group contemporaneous with the Anasazi and Hohokam. Located in south/central Arizona and New Mexico.

Morpheme: A meaningful linguistic unit that contains no smaller meaningful parts.

Motif: A design, a unit, or a pattern of design. Motifs are usually discussed as units with descriptions of how they are created and combined and what they contain within.

Nadir: Zuni directional indicator. Downward, opposite of Zenith.

Navajo: An Athapaskan people of northern Arizona and New Mexico and ranging into Colorado and Utah. The Navajo arrived late into the Southwest, approximately A.D. 1500.

Ne'wekwe: Zuni clown society. When these clowns appear in public they are striped with black and white paint. They are associated with the night sky, winter and the underworld.

Obsidian Hydration: A dating technique using the naturally occurring mineral obsidian, or volcanic glass. Obsidian was used by the prehistoric peoples to make various stone tools. When the surface of the stone is knapped or flaked, it creates a new surface which begins to soak up moisture at the fixed rate of one micron every one hundred years. This absorption can be easily measured and a date obtained for the creation of the tool.

Omauwu: Hopi "rain cloud".

Onane: Spirit break. A gap left in the design of a vessel or weaving which allows the spirit of the piece to escape.

Olla: A large ceramic jar.

Palunhoya: One of the Hopi war twins.

Paste: The body of the clay.

Patki: Second Hopi phratral organization, "cloud/house".

Petroglyph: A prehistoric symbol representation pecked or chiseled into stone.

Pictograph: A prehistoric symbol representation usually executed on stone. These representations are painted, not pecked or chiseled.

Pinedale Style: A collection of painted characteristics that are found on prehistoric ceramics that date between A.D. 1300 and A.D. 1400 including large dominating black painted motifs that are enhanced with hachured units and an increase in the use of banding to create fields of design.

Pinto: Ceramic type found primarily below the Mogollon Rim in Arizona. Bowl exteriors are slipped red and the interiors are slipped white and then painted in black. This ceramic type is the forerunner of both Gila Polychromes and Tonto Polychromes.

Pit House: An early form of architecture that was used in the southwest before A.D. 900. A shallow circular area was excavated and the roof was added using perishable materials.

Pochteca: Prehistoric traders. These wanderers traveled across the Southwest trading turquoise, copper bells and even live parrots.

Points: Small lithic tips for drills, arrows, spears, and knives.

Polish: The surface treatment of a ceramic vessel. The clay body, the slips and occasionally even the painted designs are rubbed into the surface of the vessel using a small polishing stone.

Polychrome: More than two colors. Ceramic analysis includes the background or slip color of the vessel. If a vessel has an overall red slip and is then painted in black and white, it is considered a polychrome.

Proto-historically: History, as we refer to the term, begins with written records. In the Southwest, this period begins around A.D. 1540 Spanish contact. Anything before Spanish contact is prehistoric and anything after Spanish contact is historic. Proto-historic refers to the grey area in between the two temporal designations.

Provenance: The location of an artifact.

Puerco Red Ware: A White Mountain Red Ware ceramic type dating between A.D. 1100 and A.D. 1200.

Puerco Style: A unique ceramic style that was used on prehistoric pottery between A.D. 1000 and A.D. 1200 using solid and hachured motifs that do not interlock with one another.

Puukonhoya: One of the Hopi war twins.

Rain Streamer: A symbol for rain, rainbow, or rain-bringing, found protruding from the rear of zoomorphic representations.

Relative: In regard to dating techniques. A relative date for an artifact as opposed to an absolute date, is one that was obtained by association. Two artifacts are found together on the floor of a room, one of the artifacts can be dated using absolute methods, the other cannot.

Both artifacts are assumed to have been in the room and used at the same time.

Reserve Black-on-white: A Cibola White Ware dating between A.D. 900 and A.D. 1100.

Rock Art: A term which refers to any prehistoric representation depicted on stone, be it a painted pictograph, or a pecked/chiseled petroglyph.

Rosetta Stone: A stone tablet found in 1799 that provided the first clue to deciphering Egyptian hieroglyphs. The tablet displayed the same story written in three different languages.

Scoria: An abrasive volcanic ash or cinder material.

Salado: Prehistoric culture in Arizona with a merging of Mogollon and Anasazi traits from A.D. 1100 to A.D. 1450.

Shaft Abrader: A stone with a groove or grooves used to straighten and polish the surface of an arrow shaft.

Sherd: A fragment of pottery.

Sikyatki: A prehistoric pueblo of the "firewood" people of the Hopi. Located in northeastern Arizona.

Sipapu: Passageway to the underworld in pueblo thought.

Slip: A thick soupy clay paste, sometimes colored, that is applied to a ceramic vessel before the paint is applied. The slip is rubbed into the surface of the vessel using a polishing stone.

Spirit Break: A line painted around a vessel with an unpainted area or gap in the line to allow the spirit of the vessel to emerge.

St. Johns Polychrome: A ceramic type from the White Mountain Red Ware series dating between A.D. 1175 and A.D. 1300.

Style: Regarding ceramics; a collection of traits found in the painted designs of ceramics, disregarding color, and focusing on the design layouts, fields of decoration, motifs, hachuring, framing lines, and patterns.

Talawipiki: Hopi "lightning".

Tanaka: Hopi "rainbow".

Temper: Coarse material added to clays to prevent cracking when fired. Common tempers are sand, ground pottery sherds, and shell.

Tradition: Referring to ceramic typology this simply means a group of ceramics that share common elements, such as provenance, style, and most notably a developmental sequence.

Tree-Ring Dating: An archaeological dating technique which employs the differences in the width of tree rings recovered from either beams or charcoal from a prehistoric site. Wide rings represent wetter years, narrow rings dryer years. Not all types of wood are dateable. This dating method was developed by A.E. Douglass in the 1920s, while investigating sun spots.

Tularosa Style: A recognizable collection of painted patterns that appear on prehistoric ceramics between the years of A.D. 1200 to A.D. 1300 including interlocked hachured and solid units. The hachured units are slightly larger than the solid units. The use of the interlocked hachured and solid spiral is very frequent.

Type: Referring to ceramics; a recognized collection of attributes particular to itself alone, enabling the recognition of the type in both sherd and vessel form and meaningful in terms of a specific time period and geographical area. Modal attributes differentiate one type from another.

Umtak-ina: Hopi god, "the thunder".

Vitreous: Glass-like. After A.D. 1300 copper/manganese/lead glazes were introduced in the White Mountains. These produced a shiny glaze with good color, but the glazing would tend to run during firing. This limited the controlled designs of earlier times and may have hampered the continued use of meaningful symbolism on ceramics.

White Mountain Red Wares: A ceramic tradition found in the White Mountains of Arizona, beginning with the Puerco Black-on-red ceramics around A.D. 1000 and continuing through the Fourmile and Point of Pines Polychromes to around A.D. 1450.

Whorls: A small disk with a hole at center used to stabilize the shaft of a bow or pump drill.

Wingate Black-on-red: A ceramic type from the White Mountain Red Ware series dating between A.D. 1050 and A.D. 1200.

Wingate Style: A recognizable group of painted patterns that are exhibited on prehistoric ceramics between the years A.D. 1000 and A.D. 1200 and consisting of interlocked hachured and solid units and the hachured areas are always larger than the solid units.

Yoki: Hopi "rain".

Zenith: Zuni and Hopi directional indicator. The point above, opposite of Nadir or below.

Zoomorphic: A representation that resembles an animal or has animal attributes.

Zuni: Pueblo people of Arizona and New Mexico. Possible ancestors of the prehistoric pueblo peoples. Practicing Katsina Cults.

Zuni Glaze Wares: A sequence of ceramic types beginning around the year A.D. 1300 which employ the use of a vitreous or glassy paint which runs and blurs during firing.

Bibliography

Abel, L. J.
1955   *Pottery Types of the Southwest: Wares 5A, 10A, 10B, 12A, San Juan Red Ware, Mesa Verde Gray, and White Ware, San Juan White Ware.* Museum of Northern Arizona, Ceramic Series, No. 3b, Flagstaff.

Adams, Charles E.
1991   *The Origin and Development of the Pueblo Katsina Cult.* University of Arizona Press, Tucson, Arizona.

Anderson, Keith
1971   *Excavations at Betatakin and Keet Seel.* The Kiva 37;1-29.

Aveni, A. F.
1980   *Skywatchers of Ancient Mexico.* University of Texas Press, Austin, Texas.

Barnes, F. A.
1982   *Canyon Country Prehistoric Rock Art.* Wasatch Publishers Inc. Salt Lake City, Utah.

Barnett, Franklin
1973   *Dictionary of Prehistoric Indian Artifacts of the American Southwest.* Northland Press, Flagstaff, Arizona.

Barry, John
1981   *American Indian Pottery.* Books Americana. Florence, Alabama.

Boas, Franz
1927   *Primitive Art.* H. Aschehoug and Co., Oslo. Oslo Institute for Comparative Research in Human Culture.

Brand, D.D.
1935   *The Distribution of Pottery Types in Northwestern Mexico.* American Anthropologist. n.s. Vol 37, No 2.

Brew, J. O.
1943   *On the Pueblo IV and on the Kachina-Tlaloc Relations in El Norte de Mexico y el Sur de los Estados Unidos, Tercera Reunion de Mesa Redonda sobre Problemas Antropologicas de Mexico y Centro America,* Sociedad Mexican de Antropologia (Mexico City).

Brody, J. J.
1977   *Mimbres Painted Pottery. School of American Research,* Santa Fe. University of New Mexico Press, Albuquerque.
1983   *Mimbres Pottery. Ancient Art of the American Southwest.* Hudson Hills Press, New York.

Bunzel, Ruth L.
1929   *The Pueblo Potter.* Columbia Univ. Press, N.Y.
1932   *Zuni Kachinas: An Analytical Study.* Forty-seventh Annual Report of the Bureau of American Ethnology, 1929-30. Washington D.C.

Burgh, R. F.
1959   *Ceramic Profiles in the Western Mound at Awatovi, Northeastern Arizona.* American Antiquity, Vol. 25, No. 2, Salt Lake City, Utah.

Bushnell, G. H. S.
1955   *Some Pueblo IV Pottery Types from Kechipawan, New Mexico, U.S.A.* Anais do XXXI Congresso Internacional de Americanistas, San Paulo, 1954, Vol. 2. Editora Anhembi, Sao Paulo.

Carlson, Roy L.
1970   *White Mountain Red Ware. A Pottery Tradition of East-Central Arizona and Western New Mexico.* Anthropological Papers of the University of Arizona. Number 19. The University of Arizona Press, Tucson, Arizona.

Carr, Pat
1979   *Mimbres Mythology.* Univ. of Texas, Southwestern Studies, Monograph No. 56, El Paso, Texas.
Chapman, K. M.
1933   *Pueblo Indian Pottery. Vol. I, Editions d'Art,* C. Szwedzicki, Nice, France.
Chapman, K. M./Ellis, B. T.
1951   *The Line Break, Problem Child of Pueblo Pottery.* El Palacio, Vol. 58, No. 9, Santa Fe, New Mexico.
Clarke, E. P.
1935   *Designs on the Prehistoric Pottery of Arizona.* University of Arizona Bulletin, Vol. 6, No. 4, Social Science Bulletin, No. 9 Tucson, Arizona.
Colton, H. S.
1941   *Winona and Ridge Ruin. Part II, Notes on the Technology and Taxonomy of the Pottery.* Museum of Northern Arizona Bulletin. No. 19, Flagstaff.
1952   *Pottery Types of the Arizona Strip and Adjacent Areas in Utah and Nevada.* Mus. of Northern Arizona. Ceramic Series No. 1.
Colton/Hargrave
1937   *Handbook of Northern Arizona Pottery Wares.* Museum of Northern Arizona Bull. 11.
Cordell, Linda S.
1984   *Prehistory of the Southwest.* Dept of Anthropology, University of New Mexico, Albuquerque, New Mexico. Academic Press, Inc. N.Y.
Cosgrove, H. S. and Cosgrove, C. B.
1932   *The Swarts Ruin: A Typical Mimbres Site in Southwestern New Mexico.* Papers of the Peabody Museum of Archaeology and Ethnology, vol. 15, no. 1 (Cambridge, Mass.).
Cunkle, J. R.
1993   *Talking Pots, Deciphering the Symbols of a Prehistoric People.* Golden West Publishers, Phoenix, Arizona.
Cushing, Frank H.
1882-83 *A Study of Pueblo Pottery as Illustrative of Zuni Culture Growth.* Fourth Annual Report of the Bureau of American Ethnology. Washington, D.C.
1880-81 *Zuni Fetishes.* Second Annual Report of the Bureau of American Ethnology. Washington, D.C.
1979   *Zuni.* University of Arizona Press, Tucson, Arizona.
1979   *Zuni Folk Tales.* University of Arizona Press. Tucson, Arizona.
Danson, E. B.
1957   *An Archaeological Survey of West Central New Mexico and East Central Arizona.* Papers of the Peabody Museum, Harvard Univ., Vol. 44, No. 1. Cambridge.
Dean, Jeffrey S.
1970   *Aspects of Tsegi phase social organization: a trial reconstruction.* In, *Reconstruction of Prehistoric Pueblo Societies,* edited by William A. Longacre, pp. 140-174 School of American Research, Santa Fe, and the University of New Mexico Press, Albuquerque.
Dedera, Don.
1975   *Navajo Rugs. The Northland Press,* Flagstaff, Arizona.
Di Peso, Charles
1974   *Casas Grandes: A Fallen Trading Center of the Gran Chichimeca. 3 vol.* Northland Press, Flagstaff, Arizona.
Dittert, A. E./Plog, F.
1980   *Generations in Clay, Pueblo Pottery of the American Southwest.* Northland Press.

Douglass, A. E

1929   *The Secret of the Southwest Solved by Talkative Tree Rings.* National Geographic Magazine. Vol 56, No. 6. Washington, D.C.

1938   *Southwestern Dated Ruins:V. Tree Ring Bulletin.* Vol. 5, No. 2, Flagstaff, AZ

Durkheim, Imile and Mauss, Marcel

1963   *Primitive Classification.* Chicago: University of Chicago Press.

Dutton, Bertha

1963   *Sun Father's Way: The Kiva Murals of Kuaua.* University of New Mexico Press, Albuquerque, NM.

Ellis, Florence Hawley and Hammack, Laurens

1968   *The Inner Sanctum of Feather Cave, A Mogollon Sun and Earth Shrine Linking Mexico and the Southwest.* American Antiquity 33:25-44.

Fewkes, Jesse Walter

1898   *Sityatki and It's Pottery.* Excerpt (pp. 631-728) Archeological Expedition to Arizona in 1895. Seventeenth Annual Report of the Bureau of American Ethnology to the Secretary of the Smithsonian Institution, 1895-96. Washington D.C.

1904   *Two Summers' Work in Pueblo Ruins.* 22nd Annual Report of the Bureau of American Ethnology, Part 1. Washington, D.C.

Forde, C. D.

1931   *Hopi Agriculture and Land Ownership,* Royal Anthropological Institute 61: 357-405.

Furst, Peter T.

1974a   *Ethnographic Analogy in the Interpretation of West Mexican Art.* In "The Archaeology of West Mexico" ed. Betty Bell (Ajijie, Jalisco; West Mexican Society for Advanced Study).

Gifford, J.C.

1953   *A Guide to the Description of Pottery Types in the Southwest.* Archaeological Seminar of the Department of Anthropology, University of Arizona, Spring, 1952. Tucson, Arizona.

Gladwin, W. /Gladwin H. S.

1930   *An Archaeological Survey of Verde Valley. Gila Pueblo,* Medallion Papers, No. VI, Globe, Arizona.

1930b   *Some Southwestern Pottery Types: Series I. Medallion Papers,* No. 8, Gila Pueblo, Globe, Arizona.

1931   *Some Southwestern Pottery Types: Series II. Medallion Papers,* No. 10. Gila Pueblo, Globe, Arizona.

Grant, Campbell

1981   *Rock Art of the American Indian.* Outbooks, Golden, Colorado.

Guthe, C.E.

1925   *Pueblo Pottery Making.* Papers of the Phillips Academy Southwestern Exp., No. 2, Yale Univ. Press, New Haven, Conn.

Hargrave, L. L.

1929   *Elden Pueblo. Museum of Northern Arizona,* Museum notes, Vol.2, No. 5, Flagstaff., AZ

1932   *Guide to Forty Pottery Types from the Hopi Country and the San Francisco Mountains, Arizona.* Museum of Northern Arizona, Bull. 1. Flagstaff, Arizona.

Haury, E. W. and Hargrave, L. L.

1931   *Showlow and Pinedale Ruins* in *Recently Dated Pueblo Ruins in Arizona.* Smithsonian Miscellaneous Collections, Vol. 82, No. 11, PP 4-79, No. 11, WA

Haury, Emil W.

1930   *A Sequence of Decorated Red Ware from the Silver Creek Drainage.* Museum of Northern Arizona, Museum Notes, Vol.2, No.11, Flagstaff, AZ.

1931   *Showlow and Pinedale Ruins.* Recently Dated Pueblo Ruins in Arizona. Smithsonian Miscellaneous Collections, Vol. 82. No.11 Washington.

1932   *The Age of Lead Glaze Decorated Pottery in the Southwest. American Anthropologist,* n.s., Vol. 34. Menasha.

1934   *The Canyon Creek Ruin and the Cliff Dwellings of the Sierra Ancha.* Medallion Papers, No. 14, Gila Pueblo, Globe, Arizona.

1945   *The Excavation of Los Muertos and Neighboring Ruins in the Salt River Valley, Southern Arizona.* Papers of the Peabody Museum, Harvard University, Vol. 24, No. 1, Cambridge, Mass.

1958   *Evidence at Point of Pines for a Prehistoric Migration from Northern Arizona.* In "Migrations in New World Cultural History" Univ. of Arizona Bulletin, Vol. 29, No. 2, Social Science Bulletin, No 27, Tucson, Arizona.

1978   *The Hohokam, desert farmers and craftsmen.* Excavations at Snaketown, 1964-1965. University of Arizona Press, Tucson, Arizona.

Hawley, F. M

1929   *Prehistoric Pottery Pigments of the Southwest.* American Anthropologist, n.s., Vol. 31, No. 4, pp. 731-54 Menasha.

1936   *Field Manual of Prehistoric Southwestern Pottery Types.* Univ. of N.M. Bull., Anthro. Series, Vol. 1, No. 4.

1950   *Field Manual of Prehistoric Southwestern Pottery Types,* revised edition. University of New Mexico Bulletin, Anthropological Series, Vol. 1, No. 4. Albuquerque, NM.

Hayden, Julian D.

1972   *Hohokam Petroglyphs of the Sierra Pinacate, Sonora, and the Hohokam Shell Expeditions.* The Kiva 37;74-83.

Heizer, R.

1974   *The World of the American Indian.* Washington, D.C.: The National Geographic Society.

Hibben, Frank C.

1966   *A Possible Pyramidal Structure and other Mexican Influences at Pottery Mound, New Mexico.* American Antiquity 31:552-529.

Hill, James N.

1970   *Broken K Pueblo: prehistoric social organization in the American Southwest.* Anthropological Papers of the University of Arizona 18. Tucson.

Hodge, Fredrick W.

1907-10 *Handbook of American Indians North of Mexico. Part I.* Rowman and Littlefield. Reprinted 1979 from the 30th Annual Report of the Bureau of American Ethnology, Washington, D.C.

Holmes, W. H.

1882-83 *Pottery of the Ancient Pueblos.* Fourth Annual Report to the Bureau of American Ethnology. Washington, D.C.

Hough, W.

1930   *Exploration of Ruins in the White Mountain Apache Indian Reservation.* Proceedings of the United States National Museum. 1-21, Washington, D.C.

Kabotie, Fred

1949   *Designs from the Ancient Mimbrenos with a Hopi Interpretation* (San Francisco; Grabhorn Press).

Kearns, Timothy M.

1973   *Abiotic Resources, in An Archaeological Survey of the Orme Reservoir,* assembled by Veletta Canouts and Mark Gready. Manuscript prepared for the U.S. Bureau of Reclamation, Central Arizona Project, on file at Arizona State Museum, University of Arizona (Tucson).

Kidder, Alfred Vincent
1931   *Pottery of Pecos:* Vol. I. Yale Univ. Press, New Haven.
1932   The Artifacts of Pecos, Papers of the Southwestern Expedition, no. 6, Phillips Academy (New Haven: Yale University Press).

Kidder/Shepard
1936   *The Pottery of Pecos.* Vol.2, Papers of the Phillips Academy, Southwestern Expedition, No. 7, Yale University Press, New Haven.

Kirk, R.
1943   *Introduction to Zuni Fetishism.* El palacio, Vol. L, Nos. 6, 7, 8, 9, and 10 Santa Fe, N.M.

Lang, Richard W.
1976   *An Archaeological Survey of the Upper San Cristobal Drainage, in the Galiseo Basin, Santa Fe County,* New Mexico. School of American Research (Santa Fe).

LeBlanc, Steven A.
1983   *The Mimbres People: Ancient Pueblo Painters of the American Southwest.* Thames and Hudson Inc., New York, New York.

Lister, Robert H.; Lister, Florence C.
1987   *Aztec Ruins, on the Animas, Excavated, Preserved, and Interpreted.* University of New Mexico Press. Albuquerque, New Mexico.

Lightfoot, K.G./Jewett, R.
1984   *Late Prehistoric Ceramic Distributions in East-Central Arizona: An Examination of Cibola Whiteware, White Mountain Redware, and Salado Redware. Regional Analysis of Prehistoric Ceramic Variation: Contemporary Studies of the Cibola Whitewares.* Anthropological Research Papers, No. 31. Arizona State University, Tempe, Arizona.

Longacre, W.A.
1964   *Archaeology as Anthropology.* Science 144, Washington, D.C.

Mails, Thomas E.
1983   *The Pueblo Children of the Mother Earth.* Vol. 1. Doubleday and Company, Inc. Garden City, New York.

Martin, P.S., et al
1952   *Mogollon Cultural Continuity and Change: The Stratigraphic Analysis for Tularosa and Cordova Caves.* Chicago Natural History Museum, Fieldiana: Anthro. Vol. 40.

Martin, P. S. and Rinaldo J. B.
1950   *Sites of the Reserve Phase, Pine Lawn Valley, Western New Mexico. Fieldiana:* Anthropology, Vol. 38, No 3. Chicago Natural History Museum, Chicago.

1960   *Excavations in the Upper Little Colorado Drainage,* Eastern Arizona. Fieldiana: Anthropology, Vol. 51, No. 1, Chicago Natural History Museum, Chicago.

Martin/Rinaldo/Barter
1957   *Late Mogollon Communities: Four Sites of the Tularosa Phase, Western New Mexico.* Fieldiana: Anthropology, Vol. 49. No. 1. Chicago Natural History Museum, Chicago.

Martin, P. S./Rinaldo J. B./Bluhm E. A.
1954   *Caves of the Reserve Area.* Fieldiana: Anthropology. Vol 42, Chicago Museum of Natural History, Chicago.

Martin, P.S./Rinaldo J.B./Bluhm E.A./Cutler H.C.
1956   *Higgins Flat Pueblo, Western New Mexico.* Fieldiana: Anthropology, Vol. 45, Chicago Museum of Natural History, Chicago.

Martin, P. S. /Rinaldo J. B./Longacre W. A.
1961   *Mineral Creek Site and Hooper Ranch Pueblo, Eastern Arizona.* Fieldiana: Anthropology, Vol.52, Chicago Natural History Museum, Chicago.

Martin/Willis
1940   *Anasazi Painted Pottery in the Field Museum of Natura History.* Field Museum of Natural History, Anthropological Memoirs, Vol. 5 Chicago.

Mera, H. P.
1934   *Observations on the Archaeology of the Petrified Forest National Monument.* Laboratory of Anthropology, Technical Series Bulletin No.7, Santa Fe.

Morris, E. H.
1936   *Archaeological Background of Dates in Early Arizona Chronology.* Tree Ring Bulletin, Vil. II, No. 4, Flagstaff, AZ.

1957   *Stratigraphic Evidence for a Cultural Continuum at the Point of Pines Ruin.* Master's thesis, Univ. of Arizona, Tucson.

Moulard, Barbara, L.
1984   *Within the Underworld Sky. Mimbres Ceramic Art in Context.* Twelvetrees Press, Pasadena, California 91102.

Mountjoy, Joseph B.
1974a   *Some Hypotheses regarding the Petroglyphs of West Mexico,* Mesoamerican Studies No. 9, University Museum, Southern Illinois University (Carbondale).

Nesbitt, P. H.
1938   *Starweather Ruin, A Mogollon Pueblo Site in Upper Gila Area of New Mexico.* Logan Mus. Publ. in Anthro., Bull. No. 6, Beloit, Wisc.

1939   *Starkweather Ruin: A Mogollon-Pueblo Site in the Upper Gila Area of New Mexico, and Affiliative Aspects of the Mogollon Culture.* Logan Museum Publications in Anthropology, Bulletin No. 6, Beloit.

Newcomb, F. J./ Reichard, G. A.
1975   *Sandpaintings of the Navajo Shooting Chant.* Dover Publications, Inc. New York.

Olson, A. P.
1959   *Evaluation of the Phase Concept..as Applied to 11th and 12th Century Occupations at Point of Pines, East Central, Arizona.* Univ. of Ariz. Ph.D. Dissertation

Olson, A. P./ Wasley, W. W.
1956   *An Archaeological Traverse Survey in West-Central New Mexico.* In Pipeline Archaeology. Laboratory of Anthropology, Museum of Northern Arizona, Sante Fe, and Flagstaff.

Patterson, Alex
1992   *A Field Guide to Rock Art Symbols of the Greater Southwest.* Johnson Books, Boulder, Colorado.

Peckham, Stewart
1990   *From This Earth.* Museum of New Mexico Press. Santa Fe, New Mexico.

Pike, Donald G./Muench, David.
1974   *Anasazi, Ancient People of the Rock.* Crown Publishers Inc. New York.

Plog, Stephen
1980   *Stylistic Variation in Prehistoric Ceramics.* Design analysis in the American Southwest. Cambridge University Press, Cambridge.

Rands, R. L.
1961   *Elaboration and Invention in Ceramic Traditions.* American Antiquity, Vol 26, No 3. Salt Lake City.

Reed, E. K.
1955   *Painted Pottery and Zuni History.* Southwestern Journal of Anthropology, Vol.11, No. 5, Albuquerque, New Mexico.

1977   Navajo Medicine Man Sandpaintings. Dover Publications, Inc. New York.

Rinaldo, J. B.
1959   *Foote Canyon Pueblo, Eastern Arizona.* Fieldiana: Anthropology, Vol. 49, No. 2. Chicago Natural History Museum, Chicago.

1961   *Mineral Creek Site and Hooper Ranch Pueblo,* Eastern Arizona. Fieldiana: Anthropology, Vol. 52. Chicago Natural History Museum, Chicago, Ill.

Rinaldo, J. B./ Bluhm E. A.
1956   *Late Mogollon Pottery Types of the Reserve Area.* Fieldiana: Anthropology, Vol 36, No. 7, Chicago Natural History Museum, Chicago.

Robbins R. R./Westmoreland R. B.
Unpublished. *Astronomical Imagery and Numbers in Mimbres Pottery.*

Roberts, F. H. H., Jr.
1931   *The Ruins at Kiatuthlanna, Eastern Arizona.* Bureau of American Ethnology, Bulletin 100, Washington, D.C.

1932   The Village of the Great Kivas on the Zuni Reservation, New Mexico. Bureau of American Ethnology, Bull. 111. Wash.

Sayles, E.B.
1936   *Some Southwestern Pottery Types.* Series V. Medallion Papers, No. 21, Gila Pueblo, Globe, Arizona.

Schaafsma, Polly and Curtis F. Schaafsma
1974   *Evidence for the origins of Pueblo kachina cult as suggested by Southwestern rock art.* American Antiquity 39(4):535-545.

Schaafsma, Polly.
1980   *Indian Rock Art of the Southwest.* School of American Research. Southwest Indian Arts Series. University of New Mexico Press, Albuquerque.

Schele, L.
1977   *"Palenque: the House of the Dying Sun".* Native American Astronomy, University of Texas Press, Austin, Texas.

Schmidt, E. F.
1928   *Time-Relations of Prehistoric Pottery Types in Southern Arizona.* Anthropological Papers of the American Museum of Natural History, Vol. 30, Part 5, New York

Shepard, A. O.
1936   *The Technology of Pecos Pottery. In: The Pottery of Pecos.* A.V. Kidder and A.O. Shepard, Vol. II Pt. II, Yale Univ. Press, New Haven.

1942   *Rio Grande Glaze Paint Ware: A Study Illustrating the Place of Ceramic Technological Analysis in Archaeological Research.* Carnegie Institution of Washington, Publication 528,pp 129-260. Washington.

1956   *Ceramics for the Archaeologist.* Carnegie Institution of Washington Publication 609. Washington.

Smiley, T. L.
1952   *Four Late Prehistoric Kivas at Point of Pines, Arizona.* University of Arizona Bulletin, Vol. 23, No. 3 Social Science Bulletin, No. 21, Tucson.

Smith, Watson
1952   *Kiva Mural Decorations at Awatovi and Kawaika-a with a Survey of Other Wall Paintings in the Pueblo Southwest.* Papers of the Peabody Museum, Harvard University, Vol. 37 Cambridge, Mass.

1966   *The Excavation of Hawikuh, Report of the Hendricks-Hodge Expedition 1917-1923.* Museum of the American Indian, Heye Foundation, New York.

Spier, Leslie
1917   *An Outline for a Chronology of Zuni Ruins.* Anthropological Papers of the American Museum of Natural History. Vol. 18, Part 3, New York.

1919   *Ruins of the White Mountains, Arizona.* Anthropological Papers of the American Museum of Natural History, Vol 18, Part 5, New York, NY.

Steen, Charlie R.
1966   *Excavations at Tse Ta'a, Canyon de Chelly National Monument, Arizona.* Archaeological Research Series no. 9, National Park Service (Wash. D.C.).

Sturtevant, William C.
1979   *Handbook of North American Indians, Southwest.* Vol 9. Smithsonian Institution, Washington, D.C.
Thompson, J. S. E.
1967   *Creation Myths (part 2).* Estudios de Cultura Maya. Vol. 5. Mexico City: UNAM.
Voth, H. R.
1905   *The Traditions of the Hopi,* Field Columbian Museum Publication 96, Anthropological Series vol. 8 (Chicago).
Walters, Frank
1977   *Book of the Hopi.* Penguin Books USA Inc., New York, New York.
Wasley, W. W.
1952   *Late Pueblo Occupation at Point of Pines, East Central Arizona.* M.A. Thesis, Univ. of Ariz.
1959   *Cultural Implications of Style Trends in Southwestern Prehistoric Pottery.* PhD Dissertation, Univ. of Ariz.
Wellmann, K. F.
1975   *Some Observations on the Bird Motif in North American Indian Rock Art.* Paper presented at the symposium on American Indian Rock Art (El Paso, Texas).
Wendorf, F.
1950   *A Report on the Excavation of a Small Ruin Near Point of Pines, East Central Arizona.* University of Arizona Bulletin, Vol. 21, No. 3, Social Science Bulletin No 19, Tucson, Arizona.
1953   *Archaeological Studies in the Petrified Forest National Monument.* Museum of Northern Arizona. Bulletin 27, Flagstaff, Arizona.
Wendorf, Fred and Erik K. Reed
1955   *An Alternative Reconstruction of Northern Rio Grande Prehistory.* El Palacio 62:131-73.
Wheat, J. B.
1952   *Prehistoric Water Sources of the Point of Pines Area.* American Antiquity, Vol. 17, No.3, Salt Lake City, Utah.
Whitehead, Alfred North
1927   *Symbolism: It's Meaning and Effect.* Cambridge: At the University Press.
Wilson, Thomas
1894   *The Swastika.* Smithsonian Report, U.S. National Museum.
Wissler, Clark
1966   *Indians of the United States.* Double Day and Co. Inc.   Garden City, NY.
Woodbury, Richard B. and Nathalie F. S.
1956   *Zuni Prehistory and El Morro National Monument.* Southwestern Lore, Vol 21, Boulder, Colorado.
1966   *Decorated Pottery of the Zuni Area.* Appendix II in Contributions From the Museum of the American Indian, Heye Foundation, Vol. XX, by Watson Smith. NY New York.
Wu, Hung
1985   *Bird Motifs in Eastern Yi Art.* Orientations 16.10 (Oct.   85) 34-36, figs. 9,10,11,13,15,17.
Yarrow, H. C.
1879-80 *A Study of Mortuary Customs of the North American Indians.* First Annual Report to the Bureau of American Ethnology. Washington, D.C.
Zubrow, Ezra B. W.
1972   *Carrying capacity and dynamic equilibrium in the prehistoric Southwest.* In, Contemporary archaeology, edited by Mark P. Leone, pp. 268-279. Southern Illinois University Press, Carbondale.

Index

About the Author

Since a boy on exploring adventures with his father, James Cunkle traveled into remote areas of the Southwest and discovered the West's unspoiled natural beauty. These impressions remained with James throughout his life, haunting him into adulthood.

When James was in his early teens, he would leave the East the day that school ended in June and hitchhike to the West. With a bedroll under one arm, and a suitcase swinging at his side, he crossed hundreds of miles of wilderness and discovered prehistoric caves, petroglyphs, and archaeological sites that were unrecorded.

He entered Eastern Michigan University in Ypsilanti in 1969 and completed two years of academia. Cunkle's studies focused him toward a career in teaching.

In 1971, Cunkle left Eastern Michigan and became an artist for the next ten years. He created sculptures of glass and bronze.

Adventure called and Cunkle traveled to the headwaters of the Amazon River in Columbia, where he and a team of entomologists collected insects using a portable generator and ultraviolet lights.

Cunkle became a pilot. He soloed in less than eight hours, and built and flew experimental aircraft.

He became a scuba diver, sky diver, cave spelunker, and he learned to sail.

In the 1980s, James traveled to the Yucatan jungles of Mexico to record the vanishing life ways of the Maya Indians. Also during this adventure, the team explored the depths of Mayan caves and cenotes using scuba gear and metal detectors.

Cunkle dreamed of making a personal contribution to the sciences and the study of humankind.

Toward that end, in 1988 he graduated Cum Laude and received a B.A. in Anthropology/Archaeology from Cleveland State University, Cleveland, Ohio.

During his undergraduate career, James and his colleagues published two scientific papers: *Distal Radius and Proximal Femur Fracture Patterns in the Hamann-Todd Skeletal Collection* and *An Unknown Burial Site on Kelly's Island.* The distal radius fracture study was one of the first reports to recognize the correlation between supplemental estrogen, vitamin D and calcium in older women, in order to decrease women, in order to decrease osteoporosis.

Cunkle's first book, *Talking Pots, Deciphering the Symbols of a Prehistoric People,* translated the icons found on the pottery from Raven Site Ruins. This controversial volume doubled the meaningful symbols now recognized on not only the ceramics of prehistory, but also on the rock art of the Southwest.

Author James R. Cunkle

Cunkle and his colleagues are currently working on Raven Site Ruins in northeastern Arizona at the base of the White Mountains, twelve miles north of Springerville. The site has provided the majority of the data which encompass this work.

The Raven Site, known to have had several occupations over the past 800 years, was secured by the White Mountain Archaeological Center after having been at the mercy of pots hunters.

As Coordinator and Director of Research, Cunkle, along with his wife, Carol, operate the Center, a facility open to the general public and devoted to preserving, protecting and discovering the past through education and a hands-on exposure to field archaeology.

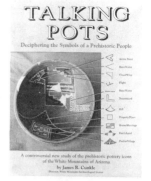

ORDER BLANK

GOLDEN WEST PUBLISHERS

✿ 4113 N. Longview Ave. • Phoenix, AZ 85014

602-265-4392 • **1-800-658-5830** • FAX 602-279-6901

Qty	Title	Price	Amount
	Arizona Adventure	6.95	
	Arizona Crosswords	4.95	
	Arizona Legends & Lore	6.95	
	Arizona Museums	9.95	
	Arizona Outdoor Guide	5.95	
	Cactus Country	6.95	
	Cowboy Slang	5.95	
	Discover Arizona!	6.95	
	Explore Arizona!	6.95	
	Fishing Arizona	7.95	
	Ghost Towns in Arizona	6.95	
	Hiking Arizona	6.95	
	Hiking Arizona II	6.95	
	Hunting Small Game in Arizona	7.95	
	Prehistoric Arizona	5.00	
	Quest for the Dutchman's Gold	6.95	
	Snakes and other Reptiles of the SW	9.95	
	Talking Pots	19.95	
	Treasures of Time	14.95	
	Verde River Recreation Guide	6.95	
Add $2.00 to total order for shipping & handling			$2.00

☐ My Check or Money Order Enclosed. . . . . $ _____

☐ MasterCard ☐ VISA

Acct. No.   Exp. Date

Signature

Name   Telephone

Address

City/State/Zip   **Call for FREE catalog**

6/94   MasterCard and VISA Orders Accepted ($20 Minimum)

Treasures

This order blank may be photo-copied.